Francis John Scott

**The light of life: sermons, preached in Holy Trinity Church,**

**Tewkesbury**

Francis John Scott

**The light of life: sermons, preached in Holy Trinity Church, Tewkesbury**

ISBN/EAN: 9783337086022

Printed in Europe, USA, Canada, Australia, Japan

Cover: Foto ©Lupo / pixelio.de

More available books at **www.hansebooks.com**

# THE LIGHT OF LIFE.

## SERMONS

PREACHED IN HOLY TRINITY CHURCH, TEWKESBURY

*Second Series.*

BY

THE REV. FRANCIS JOHN SCOTT, M.A.

(PERPETUAL CURATE.)

LONDON:
HATCHARDS, 187 PICCADILLY.
W. NORTH, TEWKESBURY.
1884.

LONDON:
PRINTED BY STRANGEWAYS AND SONS,
Tower Street, Upper St. Martin's Lane.

# PREFACE.

## ERRATA.

Page 183, line 6. *After* 'made' *insert* good.
.. 189, ,, 7. *After* 'God' *insert* and.
.. ,, .. 21. *After* 'hands,' *for* a comma *put* a period.
,. 190, .. 3. *For* 'indirect' *read* instinct.
.. ,, ,, 13. *For* 'or' *read* of.

M. E. SCOTT.

TEWKESBURY,
    *January 1st*, 1884.

LONDON:
PRINTED BY STRANGEWAYS AND SONS,
Tower Street, Upper St. Martin's Lane.

# PREFACE.

The previous volume of Sermons, entitled 'Light from the Cross,' having met with much acceptance, and many having expressed to me their high appreciation of them, I am induced to publish another Series, which I earnestly hope may be blessed of God to the manifestation of His truth, and the comfort and strengthening of His servants.

M. E. SCOTT.

Tewkesbury,
*January 1st*, 1884.

# CONTENTS.

| SERMON | | PAGE |
|---|---|---|
| I. | THE INQUIRY AND THE REPLY OF THE WATCHMAN . | 1 |

'Watchman, what of the night?'—Isa. xxi. 11, 12.

| II. | WHAT IS TRUTH? | 12 |

'What is truth?'—St. John, xviii. 38, first part.

| III. | NICODEMUS, THE TIMID DISCIPLE | 22 |

'Which at the first came to Jesus by night.'
St. John, xix., part of verse 39.

| IV. | THE ONE THING WANTING . | 35 |

'One thing thou lackest.'—St. Mark, x., part of verse 21.

| V. | FAITHFULNESS OVER FEW TALENTS | 44 |

'Faithful over a few things.'—St. Matt. xxv., part of verse 23.

| VI. | THE SIGHTS IN THE HOUSE . | 53 |

'What have they seen in thine house?'
Isa. xxxix., part of verse 4.

| VII. | THE PRESENCE OF OUR LORD AT UNITED WORSHIP | 65 |

'There am I.'—St. Matt. xviii., part of verse 20.

| VIII. | CHRIST THE FOOD OF THE SOUL: for the Holy Communion | 75 |

'Then Jesus said unto them, Verily, verily, I say unto you, Except ye eat the flesh of the Son of man, and drink His blood, ye have no life in you. Whoso eateth My flesh, and drinketh My blood, hath eternal life; and I will raise him up at the last day. For My flesh is meat indeed, and My blood is drink indeed.'
St. John, vi. 53-55.

## CONTENTS.

SERMON                                                                   PAGE

IX. SAUL THE KING, AND SAUL OF TARSUS  .  .  .   83

'And it came to pass, when all that knew him beforetime saw that, behold, he prophesied among the prophets, then the people said one to another, What is this that has come unto the son of Kish? Is Saul also among the prophets?'—1 Sam. x. 11.

'And when Saul was come to Jerusalem, he assayed to join himself to the disciples; but they were all afraid of him, and believed not that he was a disciple.'
                                        Acts, ix. 26.

X. CHRISTIAN CONFIDENCE AND CHRISTIAN DUTY  .  .  92

'Whose I am, and whom I serve.'
              Acts, xxvii., latter part of 23rd verse.

XI. NEGLECTED OPPORTUNITIES  .  .  .  .  102

'Sleep on now and take your rest.'
              St. Matt. xxvi., part of verse 45.

XII. THE REQUIREMENTS OF GOD  .  .  .  .  111

'He hath showed thee, O man, what is good; and what doth the Lord require of thee, but to do justly, and to love mercy, and to walk humbly with thy God?'
                                        Micah, vi. 8.

XIII. THE CANAANITE MOTHER  .  .  .  .  122

'O woman, great is thy faith, be it unto thee, even as thou wilt.'—St. Matt. xv., part of verse 28.

XIV. REPENTANCE: for Ash Wednesday  .  .  .  133

'For godly sorrow worketh repentance to salvation not to be repented off: but the sorrow of the world worketh death.'—2 Cor. vii. 10.

XV. THE ABSENT LORD WATCHING OVER HIS CHURCH: for Ascension Day.  .  .  .    .  .  142

'He saw them toiling in rowing.'
              St. Mark, vi., first part of verse 48.

## CONTENTS.

SERMON                                                                                       PAGE

XVI. PRAYER FOR THE HOLY GHOST: for Whit-Sunday . 152

'Take the rod, and gather thou the assembly together, thou, and Aaron thy brother, and speak ye unto the rock before their eyes: and it shall give forth his water, and thou shalt bring forth to them water out of the rock.'—Num. xx. 8.

XVII. MEMORY, AND THE WORK OF THE HOLY GHOST ON IT: for Whit-Sunday . . . . . 163

'But the Comforter, which is the Holy Ghost, whom the Father will send in my name, He shall teach you all things, and bring all things to your remembrance, whatsoever I have said unto you.'—St. John, xiv. 26.

XVIII. STEWARDSHIP . . . . . . . 174

'Give an account of thy stewardship; for thou mayest be no longer steward.'
St. Luke, xvi., last clause of verse 2.

XIX. THE SAVIOUR'S REJOICING AND ITS CAUSE . . . 183

'In that hour Jesus rejoiced in spirit, and said, I thank Thee, O Father, Lord of heaven and earth, that Thou hast hid these things from the wise and prudent, and hast revealed them unto babes, even so, Father, for so it seemed good in Thy sight.'—St. Luke, x., ver. 21.

XX. THE WORK OF THE CHURCH AND OF EACH MEMBER OF IT . . . . . . . 192

'As ye go, preach.'—St. Matt. x., part of verse 7.

XXI. THE DWELLING-PLACE OF THE LORD . . . . 205

'Will God indeed dwell on the earth? Behold, the heaven and heaven of heavens cannot contain Thee; how much less this house that I have builded?'

## CONTENTS.

| SERMON | | PAGE |
|---|---|---|
| XXII. | THE POSITION OF A TRUE CHRISTIAN, AS ILLUSTRATED BY THE POSITION OF THE HEALED DEMONIAC | 215 |

'Sitting at the feet of Jesus, clothed, and in his right mind.' St. Luke, viii., part of verse 35.

XXIII. PRAYING ALWAYS WITH ALL PRAYER AND SUPPLICATION IN THE SPIRIT . . . . . . 224

'Praying always with all prayer and supplication in the Spirit.'—Eph. vi. 18, first part.

XXIV. THE PUBLICAN'S FEAST . . . . . . 233

'And Levi made Him a great feast in his own house: and there was a great company of publicans and of others that sat down with them.'—St. Luke, v. 29.

XXV. THE LORD SHOWING TO MAN HIS THOUGHT . . 243

'He declareth unto man what is His thought.' Amos, iv., part of verse 13.

XXVI. THE DEATH OF THE RIGHTEOUS . . . . 253

'And he died.'—Gen. v. 27.

XXVII. THE LIGHT OF THE BLESSED . . . . . 263

'There shall be no night there.'—Rev. xxii. 5, first clause.

# SERMONS.

## I.

WATCHMAN, WHAT OF THE NIGHT?

Isa. xxi. 11, 12.—' Watchman, what of the night?'

THIS passage forms part of a series of prophecies. And these prophecies foretell calamities on various nations of the east and south. The assailants would represent the great empires that in succession arose and fell in the regions of the Tigris and the Euphrates, viz., Assyria, Babylon, and Persia. Among these nations we find the Edomites, the warlike inhabitants of Mount Seir, where the remains of their rock-hewn strongholds and cities still tell of their importance and fancied security. Though descendants of Abraham, and of one blood and race with the children of Israel, they were generally to be found among their most determined enemies. In the afflictions and overthrow of Jerusalem they rejoiced; but their own time of trouble was at hand, and they had in their turn to endure the woes of subjugation. When threatened by powerful foes, they are represented by Isaiah as calling upon the prophets of Israel, the messengers of their fathers' God, whom they had so long forsaken. In the darkness of terror and uncertain apprehension they send, crying, 'Watchman, what of the night? Watchman, what of the night?' What have we to fear, what to expect? Is there a morning? The prophet is directed to reply, in words of solemn warning, yet full of tender mercy, invitation, and encouragement: 'The watchman said, The morning cometh, and also the night; if ye will inquire, inquire ye: return, come.'

'The morning cometh.' Beyond the darkness that at present hangs over Israel I see the dawn of hope arising over the distant hills. I see mercy and restoration in store for the people of God. Through the long vista of ages I behold the rising of the Sun of Righteousness, the coming of Messiah, to His Temple.

'The morning cometh.' But also the night, the darkness of destruction to the enemies of God and His servants, the overthrow of the nations who set themselves against Israel. Be wise in time, if you are really desirous to know the will and purposes of God, He is ready to answer you: 'If ye will inquire, inquire ye: return, come.' Return to Israel and to Israel's God.

Come to Zion; join yourselves to the servants of Jehovah, and share in the blessings He hath reserved for them, and in the morning of prosperity that already dawns for them. The Edomites neglected the warning; they refused the invitation. Little more than one hundred years passed, when the voice of the watchman was heard again. Ezekiel had by this time taken up the watch of his departed predecessor. The Edomites, refusing to return to Zion as servants of Jehovah, had purposed to take possession of His land for themselves during the captivity of Israel and Judah in the land of Assyria and in Babylon. God sent them this message: 'Because thou hast said, These two nations and these two countries shall be mine, and we will possess it, whereas the Lord was there; thou shalt know that I am the Lord, and that I have heard all thy blasphemies which thou hast spoken against the mountains of Israel, saying, They are laid desolate, they are given us to consume. Thus saith the Lord God, When the whole earth rejoiceth, I will make *thee* desolate. Thou shalt be desolate, O mount Seir, and all Idumea, even all of it; and they shall know that I am the Lord.' (Ezek. xxxv. 10, 12, 14, 15.)

The night has come upon Edom; at this time Seir is a desolation. The Edomites have passed away, none are left; a few savage Arabs roam over the hills, and exact from the daring traveller a high price for suffering him to gaze on the ruins of the empty cities and dreary wastes of Idumea or Dumah.

I think that in applying the text for our own instruction, as we are by God's word warranted in doing, we have our attention directed to the ministers of Christ. We are set as watchmen for the people with man's approval. You do by your coming here, and listening to that which we say in our Master's name,—you do, as it were, set your seal upon our office; you choose and acknowledge us as watchmen for you in things that concern God, the soul, and eternity. Your coming to this house of God is as the cry of inquirers to the prophets: 'Watchman, what of the night? Watchman, what of the night?' But though men accept us as watchmen on their behalf, we are not so made by man's appointment. Our appointment, our commission, is from God; we receive it outwardly from those who in succession have received it through the Apostles from Christ Himself. Woe to us if we have taken on us so solemn a charge without being inwardly moved by the Holy Ghost thereto! This is our Master's command to each of us: 'Son of man, I have made thee a watchman unto the house of Israel; therefore hear the word at my mouth, and give them warning from me.

When I say unto the wicked, Thou shalt surely die; and thou givest him not warning, nor speakest to warn the wicked from his wicked way, to save his life; the same wicked man shall die in his iniquity; but his blood will I require at thine hand. Yet if thou warn the wicked, and he turn not from his wickedness, nor from his wicked way, he shall die in his iniquity; but thou hast delivered thy soul. Again, When a righteous man doth turn from his righteousness, and commit iniquity, and I lay a stumblingblock before him, he shall die : because thou hast not given him warning, he shall die in his sin, and his righteousness which he hath done shall not be remembered; but his blood will I require at thine hand. Nevertheless if thou warn the righteous man, that the righteous sin not, and he doth not sin, he shall surely live, because he is warned; also thou hast delivered thy soul.' (Ezek. iii. 17–21 and Ezek. xxxiii. 7–9.) It is this word we are to speak, and not our own. Our resolution must be that of the prophet Habakkuk (ii. 1) : 'I will stand upon my watch, and set me up upon the tower, and will watch to see what He will say unto me, and what I shall answer when I am reproved.' If, as St. Paul was, any of us are made able ministers of the new testament, we are so made by God. 2 Cor. iii. 5 : 'Not that we are sufficient of ourselves to think anything as of ourselves; but our sufficiency is of God.' Our responsibility is to God; we watch for souls, as they that must give account (Heb. xiii. 17).

Brethren, it is not an undue assumption of authority when I say that you ought first to try our words whether they be of God; and this you must do by comparing them with Holy Scripture. And if we are found true and faithful, *then*, unworthy as of ourselves we are, yet is it your duty to give heed to our warnings and exhortations during the dark and uncertain night of this our life below. If the host does not stand to arms when, quick and sharp, the challenge of the sentinel is heard, and the alarm is transmitted from post to post, their blood is upon their own heads.

'Watchman, what of the night? Watchman, what of the night?' The inquiry is here made by those who represent such as we should now call 'the unconverted.'

My brethren, do not misunderstand me as if I set myself up as a saint, and set down the greater part of you as heathens. I am not here to exalt myself or to reproach you. Yet if you will look to the word of God for the description of them that have found salvation through Jesus Christ, many of you will confess that you do not answer to that description.

Have you truly repented you of sins past, being earnestly desirous to be free from the power of sin and to be made such as God would have you to be? Have you laid the burden of sin upon Him who suffered for it on the cross? Have you believed God's promise to forgive all who plead in prayer this sacrifice of Christ as the reason why they should be forgiven? Did you ever with all your heart bow down before God and tell Him this and ask for mercy, believing that He would grant it you? Are you, in reliance on the Holy Ghost's power, trying to keep God's commandments, to put down your own evil thoughts, tempers, and desires? When God's will and your own are opposed, do you try to choose His will and to obey it? Do you know anything of the love of Christ in your hearts, and has that love been so poured into them by the Holy Spirit as to fill you with love to all, especially to them that love Him? Is the Bible very dear to you; do you study it and think over it? Do you pray, at all seasons, on every occasion? Is prayer your habit? If not, whatever may be the excellency of your character in a worldly sense, you are yet unconverted; and as such it is my duty to speak to you. Yet by your coming here you say to the minister of Christ, 'Watchman, what of the night? Watchman, what of the night?' What shall our answer be? 'The morning cometh, and also the night.' The morning of the resurrection, the morning of glory, the dawning of the everlasting day, when all believers, up-springing from the grave, joined to them which are alive and remain, shall take their place at the right hand of the Judge. The morning cometh when they shall enter into the joy of their Lord; when they shall go in with Him and be made perfectly like Him, and go no more out; when they shall begin their endless service of praise and gladness—God shall wipe away all tears from their eyes. And all this not for their sakes, but for His sake who loved them and gave Himself for them, and in whom while on earth they put their trust.

> 'The morning shall awaken,
>   The shadows pass away,
> And each true-hearted servant
>   Shall shine as doth the day.
> Exult, O dust and ashes,
>   The Lord shall be thy part;
> His only, His for ever,
>   Thou shalt be, and thou art.'

'The morning cometh, and also the night.' Yes, there is a coming night, the blackness of darkness for ever, the darkness of the soul, the darkness of despair, the darkness of them that are punished with everlasting destruction from the presence of the Lord; into which they must go that have refused Christ as their Saviour, and those that have made a false profession of faith in Him; who profess that they know God but in works deny Him, and those that have neglected His offered grace. The careless and worldly, the disobedient, the profligate, the drunkard, the liar,—all who knew their Lord's will and did it not,—' And these shall go away into everlasting punishment, but the righteous into life eternal.' (St. Matt. xxv. 46.)

O brethren, who know that you are not at peace with God, and you, who doubt whether your hearts are right in His sight; by your presence here you seem to ask, ' Watchman, what of the night?' Yet only a few ask in earnest, too many scarcely care to listen to the reply: ' The morning cometh, and also the night' —cometh swiftly, quietly, imperceptibly, hasting on with ' silent speed.' ' Awake, thou that sleepest,' before it be too late. ' If ye will inquire, inquire ye.' Only come in deep submission to God, earnestly desirous to yield unreserved obedience to His reply, and be sure that you will have a merciful response.

One came to inquire who to that day had been full of hardness of heart and unbelief. Ignorant as to the person and existence of his

Divine Redeemer, supposing the Saviour of Christians to be but a dead man, 'Who art Thou, Lord?' he inquired, and had not to *wait* for the reply: 'I am Jesus.' Another inquired of his Bible, but understood not what he read; and God answered *him* by sending Philip, who preached unto him Jesus. A third, till evening a fierce persecutor, at midnight inquired in an agony of terror, 'What must I do to be saved?' How blessed the instant reply: 'Believe on the Lord Jesus Christ, and thou shalt be saved.' 'Seek, and *ye* shall find; knock, and it shall be opened unto you.'

If ye, brethren, will inquire as these did, 'inquire ye; return, come.' Return to Him to whom in your infancy you were presented in Holy Baptism, but from whom you have wandered very far away. To-day come in humble, believing prayer, and ask him to supply each want of your souls. Hear His voice: 'Come unto Me, all ye that labour and are heavy laden, and I will give you rest.' 'The Spirit and the bride say, Come; and let him that heareth say, Come; and let him that is athirst come; and whosoever will let him take the water of life freely.' I stand as watcher for your souls; I stand at the foot of the cross. There I trust, sinner as I am, I have found mercy and cleansing in the precious blood of the Son of God. Thence alone do I dare re-echo the Saviour's invitation, Come. Calvary is my watch-tower; thence I bid each fellow-sinner, each one passing, as I am, to his grave, and after that to the judgment of Christ. I bid each in my Master's name; I beseech you in His stead; I pray you by the value of your souls, by the length of eternity, by the pain of hell, by the joy of heaven, by the blood of Christ, by the love of God, come. 'If ye will inquire, inquire ye; return, come,' for He hath said, 'Him that cometh unto Me I will in no wise cast out.'

## II.

### WHAT IS TRUTH?

St. John, xviii. 38, first part.—'What is truth?'

A QUESTION put by Pilate, in a kind of contemptuous despair; but also one that suggests itself to the minds of many as of the deepest possible importance, and therefore a question that, when put in a candid, earnest spirit, demands a solemn and careful reply.

I am not now about to speak of truth upon general subjects,—of political truth, or philosophical truth, or historical truth;—I am sent here to speak of truth as it concerns that which God has to do with man, and man with God; of truth on the subject of *religion*. Yet, *much* that must be said on the subject of religious truth, refers also to truth in general, applies equally to truth upon every subject.

Truth itself is necessarily consistent with itself.

We shall start with this principle—Two things cannot be true at one and the same time, if they contradict each other. Hence, truth does not depend on man's opinion; it is not truth merely because man thinks it to be true. Truth is something as it were outside the mind of man, something that would still be true, even though no man believed it to be so. If truth were merely that which a man thinks to be true on any subject, there could be no such thing as truth, since men hold the most contradictory opinions upon almost every conceivable subject. How, then, is man to find out truth?—especially upon the subject of religion, which is of greater importance than truth upon temporal subjects, in proportion as *Eternity* is of more importance than time.

My brethren, truth must be *revealed* to us, it must come from outside of our own minds, from One who sees things as they are, and Who has no interest in deceiving us. It must come to us from God. Has such an one ever revealed truth to man? truth as concerns *Himself*, and *ourselves*, truth as concerns our condition here, and our lot for the future? Christianity replies in the affirmative. There is a certain amount of religious truth revealed to us in the world around us, being understood by the things which we see, and hear, and feel. This is what we call the truth, or truths of natural religion; and these truths may be known, and learned, of all men who honestly set themselves to discover them: so says St. Paul (Rom. i. 19, 20). And conscience in each reflecting man agrees to this, and bears witness that it is so. But in the present state of mankind, this revelation has not proved sufficient. By its aid man *might* have felt after, and have found God, *might* do so now. But, alas! they *have not* done so, and never will.

A further revelation of religious truth from God was necessary, and that too has been given to man—either by convictions impressed upon the hearts of men bearing witness to the truth, as concerning God, and his mind and will towards man, and accompanied by the assurance that they were so impressed on the soul by God Himself; or by a voice from the sky, heard by the outward ear, or by writings actually delivered from the clouds, into the hand of man; or by that visible appearance and audible conversation of the Divine Person in human form, or of a messenger sent from the other world. In all these various ways, during a long course of ages, God was pleased to reveal truth to mankind. And here I may be met by the question, 'How are we to know that the impressions on men's minds, of which you speak, did really come from God? How are we to know that the voices they heard were not delusions, and that the persons whom they saw were any more than human beings, like themselves, mere pretenders to divinity, or to angelic power and commission? May not revealed truth, of which you speak, be, after all, nothing more than the *opinions* of *men*, of which you have just said that they cannot be depended on as a testimony to truth, especially truth concerning the invisible God, His will, mind, and purpose, towards man?' I reply, first, that these revelations have in them one mark which I have already pointed out to you as a necessary accompaniment of truth. A system of falsehood *may* be consistent, a system of truth *must* be consistent in all its parts—consistent with itself; no one part can contradict another.

Now, this series of revelations from God to man, made at sundry times and in divers manners, to various classes, nations, tribes, and ages, and covering a period of thousands of years, is in the most convincing way consistent with itself. It all agrees together; so much so, that those who carefully read it, as it has been recorded, cannot help seeing that its Author is One and the same, and that as He made this series of revelations, from time to time, through so long a period—thousands of years—He must have been One whose existence could not be measured by the years of human life; He must, at least, have been more than man. I reply again to the objector, that this series of revelations displays such a suitableness to the mental wants and spiritual cravings of the human race, such an universal adaptation to the necessities of all mankind in all ages, such a knowledge of the thoughts and wishes of the human heart, not merely of the heart of man in general, but of each individual soul, as to forbid us to believe it possible that they could have proceeded from any man, or set of men, or from any one but the Creator of man's body, soul, and spirit, even from God Himself.

But, above all, I would remind the objector that the giving of this series of revelations was accompanied by a set of proofs of the most wonderful kind, proofs that they had not their origin in the minds of those to whom they were made; but that they came from outside of this world, and were given by God. For to those to whom these revelations were given, and who were entrusted with the duty of publishing them, were also given powers such as none in this world possessed. They could, and did foretell things coming to pass, sometimes during their own lives, at others, long ages afterwards; and their predictions were fulfilled.

One of them was seen for a hundred and twenty years, engaged in the gradual construction of a huge vessel, while he denounced destruction at the end of that time upon a wicked world. A hundred and twenty years passed, the flood came, and he and his family floated safely upon the waters.

Another denounced plague after plague upon a cruel nation and their tyrant king, and plague after plague fell on them, until that the fear and dread came of the Exodus — the great cry throughout the land of Egypt, because in each Egyptian house the parents' hope, the first-born child, lay dead. The men to whom revelations were made had power at the same time given to perceive the secrets of men's minds at a distance, to turn seas from their bed, and rivers from their course, to stay the sun in his journey, and the moon in her nightly round, to forbid, or bring down rain, to inflict death by a word, to call back the dead out of the other world, to depart into that world visibly in a chariot of flame.

Brethren, surely they gave sufficient proof that the revelations they published truly came from the other world ; that they were what they professed to be, the unveiling by Himself, of God's mind and will to man—His *truth*. And these revelations written down for our use are what is meant by the expression, the Word of God, of which our Lord said, as it were anticipating the reply to Pilate's question, 'What is truth?' 'Thy word is truth.'

c

Such was, for ages, God's revelation of truth to man; enough to guide him through time to a happy, glorious eternity; yet, having in it from first to last this remarkable feature, that with uniform purpose, the whole series of which it consisted seemed to point to a clearer, brighter manifestation of truth to the world. Prophecies, types, laws, sacrifices, poems, histories, revealing enough of truth to save, yet so evidently led on to some further display of truth not yet made, that even they to whom these revelations were made inquired of the Giver as to this hidden meaning, this further purpose (1 Pet. i. 10, 12). Believers in the first revelation waited long and anxiously for the coming manifestation; even throughout the heathen world there was a very general expectation of the approach of some great messenger of goodness and truth from God to man. At length it came, 'in the fulness of time,' when God saw fit; and waiting believers cried, 'Lord, now lettest Thou Thy servant depart in peace, according to Thy word.'

There might seem to be a something wanting in the earlier series of revelation of truth. They presented truth in its sterner aspect. In varied form, yet was truth for the most part set before man by precept, threatening, and command. True, there was a clue of mercy running through it all, the golden thread of promise; and they who laid hold thereof were thereby guided to the milder side of truth, and found their hearts softened and sanctified by the view of pardoning, saving goodness, which the Holy Ghost, the great Revealer, enabled them to behold. But the time arrived when hope was realised, and prophecy and promise fulfilled; when religious truth was exemplified in the life and death of a *man*; when God made all truth as to Himself, and His heart and will towards us, so plain that it could be no plainer, for *God Himself* came down to dwell among us, 'God was manifest in the flesh.'

And now were shown the glory, the power, the wisdom, the justice of God, all in such a way as not only to be clear to the mind even of a little child, but to touch the heart, and affect the feelings, of sinful man; for all these were shown to man in one living, breathing, human form, and that form was a form of Love. Angels came down to adore, and celebrate this personal revelation of the truth concerning God—they filled the dark arch of the nightly sky with their brilliant forms of light, and sang the song the watching shepherds heard, 'Glory to God in the highest, and on earth peace, goodwill toward men.'

And now, brethren, if we, the messengers of God, are inquired of as to religious realities, and are asked the question in the text, 'What is truth?' our answer is in the words of St. John the Baptist, 'Behold the Lamb of God!' Ask now for truth as to your present state. We answer, 'Look to the sufferings of your sinless Lord; they will tell you of *your* sin, of what *you* deserved, of what *you* must have suffered, but for Him.' Lord, what wilt Thou have me to do?' Behold the life of Christ! hear Him say, 'Follow me.' Does God love me? Behold the crucified, dying, bleeding Lamb! He was God, and His love to you led Him so to die for you. Oh, what a sight of Divine love that dying Lord displayed? May the sight be imprinted on our hearts by the Holy Ghost.

Do you ask for truth as to the power of this sacrifice to save you, to bring you again from the grave, to give you immortal life and glory? Behold the truth in that mangled form, pierced to the heart, indisputably dead,—the truth in that cold body, laid, as yours will be, in the grave; the truth in that new-risen Lord, crying with gladdening voice, 'All hail!' to His people; the truth in that ascending Man going up to glory in the cloud; the truth, as Stephen saw it, in that Son of Man, standing at the right hand of God; the truth proclaimed by His voice on earth (St. John, xiv. 2, 3): 'I go to prepare a place for you; and if I go and prepare a place for you, I will come again and receive you unto

Myself: that where I am there ye may be also'—and declared by His voice from Heaven (Rev. i. 17, 18): 'Fear not; I am the First and the Last; I am He that liveth and was dead; and, behold! I am alive for evermore.'

Yes, brethren, this is truth; learn it in His word; study the life of the Lord Jesus; behold God your Father in Christ; take Him for your own. 'Believe on the Lord Jesus Christ and be saved.' Hear the answer to my text in St. John, xiv. 6, 'I am the Way, the Truth, and the Life; no man cometh unto the Father but by Me.'

## III.

### NICODEMUS THE TIMID DISCIPLE.

St. John, xix., part of ver. 39.—'Which at the first came to Jesus by night.'

THERE is no sentence or expression in the word of God that has not its meaning and value; nothing inserted merely for the sake of ornament or to fill up a period. When, therefore, we find any repetition of a sentence, particularly in the same book and by the same writer, we are warranted in concluding that it contains a meaning of special significance—a meaning that is to be the object of our more especial attention. Such I believe to be the case with the sentence I have read to you. Nicodemus is thrice, and thrice only, mentioned in Holy Scripture. His history is to be found only in the Gospel according to St. John. The other evangelists do not speak of him. St. John, who seems to have written for the purpose of telling us many things that the other evangelists had left out,—St. John, who, from his intimate personal friendship with the man Christ Jesus, had his memory so stored with the many other things which Jesus did that he could only make a selection from them for our use, since he says, in Eastern phraseology, 'If they should be written every one, I suppose that even the world itself could not contain the books that should be written' (St. John, xxi. 25),— St. John relates the story of Nicodemus, and *each time* that he refers to him he reminds us that he speaks of the ruler who ' at the first came to Jesus by night.'

If, brethren, you will be at the pains to search out in this Gospel the various passages which are left untold by the first three evangelists, your eyes will be opened to the wonderful value of St. John's narrative. You will be introduced to scenes of the most touching beauty, illustrating the exquisite attractiveness of our Redeemer's personal character. You will be more deeply impressed from His own teaching with the great truth that Jesus of Nazareth publicly and authoritatively claimed equality with the Father, and proclaimed Himself to be very God of very God. So that there is no *via media* of faith to be permitted. You must either deny the truthfulness and integrity of Christ, or confess that Jesus Christ is Lord, to the glory of God the Father.

Let us now return to the history of this man ' who at the first came to Jesus by night.' He was a man of learning, acquainted with the Scriptures of the Old Testament, entering but little into their deep spiritual meaning, yet well taught in the letter of God's word. We are sure of this, for he was a master (διδάσκαλος) of Israel, says our Lord. He would be well aware of the promise of a deliverer made to the fathers, and from his conduct I think we may see that he shared in the general expectation that the advent of that deliverer was at hand.

Nicodemus was also a man of high position in the Jewish government. He was a ruler (ἄρχων) of the Jews, by which expression we understand a member of the Sanhedrim, or great council of the nation. He would therefore, in all probability, be a rich man, as was the case with another of these rulers spoken of in St. Luke xviii., and as we may perhaps gather from the weight of spices which he brought for the embalming of the dead body of the Lord. A cautious, reserved, and thoughtful person, having a desire to know and do the will of God, yet, like his companion Joseph of Arimathea, much hindered in the right way, by that fear of man which bringeth a snare. He had a clear understanding of the purpose and value of miracles, as the natural authentication of a doctrine professing to be derived from the world above: 'Rabbi, we know that Thou art a Teacher come from God, for no man can do these miracles that Thou doest except God be with him' (St. John, iii. 2). With this conviction impressed upon his conscience by the Holy Ghost, he cannot rest until he has ascertained what it is that this Teacher has come to tell, and whether the message contains anything relating to himself in his public or private capacity.

Brethren, an earnest and simple desire to learn the mind and will of God is one of the best signs of the working of Divine grace in the soul of man. God give us grace to go to the Scriptures with prayer; not to make objections, not to find texts that may confirm us in our own opinions, but in the spirit of the Psalmist: 'Teach me, O Lord, the way of Thy statutes; teach me good judgment and knowledge' (Ps. cxix. 33, 66). So far it was well with Nicodemus, but now the tempter, fearing lest he should lose his prey, suggests to him the thought of his dignity, of the loss of reputation that he will incur; what a confession of ignorance will it be! What will his brother rulers, and magistrates, and teachers say of him? What a talk there will be at rich men's tables when it becomes known that Nicodemus the councillor hath sought out the lowly Jesus, to learn from Him the will of God!

Brethren, this is not the trial of the great

man alone. How many in the middle and labouring classes feel with Nicodemus! If I read my Bible, and am known to attend God's house of prayer, and to be inquiring after the way of salvation, what will they say in the neighbourhood, in the workshop, on the ship's deck, or in the barrack-room?

'Jesus, and shall it ever be
A mortal man ashamed of Thee?'

I read once of a child who had made a step beyond Nicodemus, wise as *he* thought himself— a naval volunteer, who on the first night that he spent on board his ship kneeled down to his chest to pray; amid the ridicule of his comrades owning his Lord. Nicodemus was ashamed, and, it may be, afraid, and so he came to Jesus by night. It would be a very beautiful and a very solemn sight to look on and see the meeting, probably in some very humble room just lighted by one of the dim oil lamps used in ancient days. On one side the lowly Jesus of Nazareth, in whom, nevertheless, dwelt the fulness of the Godhead bodily; on the other, the earnest, anxious face of the man aroused by the Holy Ghost, desirous to be taught of God, yet ashamed of the Teacher whom God had sent. *Humanly* speaking, we would expect to find the inquirer dismissed with the sentence : 'Whosoever shall be ashamed of Me and of My words in this adulterous and sinful generation, of him also shall the Son of man be ashamed when He cometh in the glory of His Father, with the holy angels.' (St. Mark, viii. 38.)

No, brethren, this sentence is reserved for those of us who *know* the truth and yet are ashamed to confess Christ before men. How great the gentleness of the Lord to such as with fear, it may be sinful fear of man in their hearts, are yet *seeking* to know His will. *Whenever* they seek, *however* they seek, His promise is kept : ' Seek, and ye shall find ;' ' Him that cometh unto Me I will in no wise cast out.'

So it was in the case before us. The flax was smoking, the Lord would not quench it. Nicodemus came, probably expecting some intelligence as to the kingdom of God and the coming of a triumphal Saviour on the earth. He hears from Christ the *gospel;* that man is to be saved, not by outward means or observances ; that he must pass through the mighty change of the new birth, and be made by the Holy Ghost a new creature : ' Except a man be born again, he cannot see the kingdom of God ;' that this change is wrought inwardly by Almighty power, but is to be judged of in its effects : ' The wind bloweth where it listeth, and thou hearest the sound thereof, but canst not tell whence it cometh and whither it goeth; so is every one that is born of the Spirit' (ver. 8); that a man must confess Christ before men, receiving the grace of God *through* the outward ordinances of religion : 'Except a man be born of water and of the Spirit he cannot enter into the kingdom of God' (ver. 5); that the sinner is to be saved, not by works of his own but by the suffering of another—another who is lifted up on the cross to suffer, lifted up in the gospel to be received by the penitent, lifted up in glory everlasting, for the suffering of death : 'As Moses lifted up the serpent in the wilderness, even so must the Son of man be lifted up' (ver. 14); that the means whereby we receive the benefit of this salvation is faith, and the source and fountain of this salvation is the love of God, and the extent of this salvation universal : 'For God so loved the world, that He gave His only-begotten Son, that whosoever believeth in Him should not perish, but have everlasting life.' (ver. 16.)

Nicodemus came to learn something in addition to his present faith, and moral practice, and outward observance,—Christ preached to him *Himself* and the work of the Holy Ghost : 'I am the way, the truth, and the life,' was *then*, as

## NICODEMUS THE TIMID DISCIPLE. 29

always, the sum and substance of His teaching. Nicodemus departs silenced. All this is very wonderful to him; he will go away and think over it. Most likely he found it unpleasant, not what he expected to hear. He would have liked to forget it. It must have seemed unreasonable to him that *he*, a teacher of Israel, *he*, a ruler of the Jews, a good man in the eyes of his neighbours, must become a new creature and be saved by no goodness of his own, but by faith in One who was to be crucified for him; that he could not even turn his own heart to God, but must needs be turned by a power not his own. Must his learning and dignity, his worth and reputation, all be cast down in the dust before this humble Teacher from Galilee, who foretold His own crucifixion? And so he departs by night, as he came.

Probably the rest of the disciples who had forsaken all to follow the Lord Jesus, if they knew of this visit, thought lightly of the visitor and never expected to see him more. Indeed, Nicodemus was very deficient; he lost many an opportunity of service and of self-devotion. Let none of us be contented to follow religion in secret, to hide our faith in Christ, to say, I can read and pray in private, and so avoid the reproach of the cross. God give us grace to follow the example of those who rejoiced that they were counted worthy 'to suffer shame for His name.' Yet let us be merciful in our judgment of others. Never let us despise one who comes to Jesus, even though he come to Jesus by night. God has His own way of leading each one to Himself. Nicodemus departs. The arrow of conviction is in his heart. How many a restless hour of contest between conviction and false shame and coward fear he must have spent! One day there comes before the council a question connected with the very teacher from whom he had learned such strange and startling truths. Nicodemus is in his place. He hears of a new and wondrous miracle, worked by Jesus of Nazareth. He hears Him condemned unheard, and a curse pronounced on such as follow Him. *Humanly* speaking, again, we should have expected that this fresh manifestation of enmity to Christ on the part of the upper classes among the Jews would have for ever silenced the timid disciple, and for the rest of his life driven him away from Christ. Learn and own the power of Divine grace, and see how God can overrule the schemes of Satan, and make them contribute to His own glory and His people's good. What the miracles and popularity, for a time, of Christ did not effect, was brought about by the scorn and malice of His enemies. Nicodemus is *yet* fearful; *yet* would he escape reproach for Christ's sake. Even when he stands up to speak on His behalf he does not mention the name of the despised and rejected one. But there is such grace in his heart that he cannot sit in silence, and hear Him condemned. He rises and appeals for Christ, to the principles of justice, to the rules of the law. 'Nicodemus saith unto them (*he that came to Jesus by night being one of them*), Doth our law judge any man before it hear him, and know what he doeth?' (St. John, vii. 51.) His appeal is of no avail. But the reproach which he dreads falls on him: 'They answered and said unto him, Art thou also of Galilee? Search and look, for out of Galilee ariseth no prophet.' (St. John, vii. 52.) There is no escape from the reproach of Christ. In one form or other it is sure to fall on all who, even *timidly*, yet *sincerely*, advocate His cause; therefore, brethren, be by grace *bold* and *fearless* on the Lord's side.

The council broke up, and every man went unto his own house. Nicodemus, no doubt, sad at heart, for his own half-fearful advocacy of the right; for we can see that the smoking flax shows sparks of fire now. His Lord, nevertheless, remembered the poor, timid service that he had rendered, and despised it not. It is recorded in His gospel for a memorial of him. Grieved, too, Nicodemus would be by the undisguised contempt of those with whom he had sat so long side by side in the council-chamber and on the judgment-seat. So he is silenced, and for a time we hear no more of him. Soon, however, a day arrives, a day of trial indeed—the hour of evil men, the coming in might of the prince of this world, the power of darkness. The council has met—I know not if Nicodemus was among them; we do not hear his voice. Jesus of Nazareth, bound, beaten, reviled, they have delivered up to Pilate. Scourged and crowned with thorns, He has died the death of a malefactor on the cross. Now, surely, Satan conceives that the soul of that fearful disciple is his own. He will never own in death the Lord whom in life he was afraid to confess. But, strange, wonderful, and glorious, the death of Christ brings life to Nicodemus! Was not this the thought of his heart when he heard the news? 'Jesus dead! lifted up on the cross! It is, then, as He told me so long ago,—He is a Prophet indeed. That also must be true which He said, that all who would believe in Him should be saved. I *do* believe: He *is* the Son of God. How this is to end I cannot tell, but I will trust Him now. Was He not afraid to *die* for me, and have I been afraid to own Him as my Lord? Would that I had defended Him before the council, even if I had been condemned with Him! I will fear no more. It is late to own Him, but now, at last, I *will* own Him.' Satan is defeated, grace hath conquered; the smoking flax which the loving Lord would not quench burns brightly; love and gratitude have kindled it; the breath of the Holy Ghost hath fanned it into flame. In the presence, probably, of his sneering fellow-rulers, fearless of the guard of heathen soldiers around the crosses, comes Nicodemus; his heart hath filled his hands, he brings a great burden of spices. St. John says (with holy joy at the change), ' Joseph of Arimathea, a disciple of Jesus, but secretly for fear of the Jews, besought Pilate that he might take away the body of Jesus, and Pilate gave him leave. He came, therefore, and took the body of Jesus. And there came also Nicodemus, *which at the first came to Jesus by night*, and brought a mixture of myrrh and aloes, about an hundred pound weight. Then took they the body of Jesus, and wound it in linen clothes, as the manner of the Jews is to bury.' (St. John, xix. 38-40.)

And so the Lord triumphed, and took with Him to Paradise, as a proof of His victory, the saved soul of a crucified thief, and left behind Him, in token of the power of His grace, His two fearful, secret disciples, reverently, lovingly, courageously, openly, bearing His dead body to the grave,—men whose cowardice overcame their convictions till His dying love conquered their fears, till they were converted at the cross,—

'The wondrous cross
On which the Prince of glory died.'

## IV.

### THE ONE THING WANTING.

St. Mark x., part of ver. 21.—'One thing thou lackest.'

THERE is an expression very frequently used by our Lord to denote the rule under which alone a man can be safe for time or for eternity—the kingdom of God or of heaven. The words are full of meaning; they signify the rightful claims of the Divine Sovereign, the King eternal, immortal, invisible, the only wise God, and the true position of man. Subjection of body, soul, and spirit in implicit, unswerving obedience to His authority. The duty of man to God is not obedience to God so far as such obedience commends itself to his moral sense, and so far as God's commands appear to him to be good and right. Man's duty to God is to ascertain to the best of his ability what the will of God *is*, and then simply and instantly to comply. Should any command of God appear unreasonable or even wrong, it is, nevertheless, his duty to submit, assured that the All-wise

Creator knows best what is good, and holy, and true. Further, this obedience, this submission, admits of no exception. He that offends in one point is guilty of all. Even in an earthly kingdom that subject who in one thing refuses obedience, however dutiful in other respects, is deservedly treated as a rebel.

The words I have chosen as a text are part of our Saviour's reply to one who sought entrance into the kingdom of God,—a young and wealthy man who came to Him inquiring the way to obtain life everlasting. There was much that was interesting and attractive in his character, and in his present application to Christ. He was earnest, humble, and sincere. He came running to Jesus, as in fear lest he should miss the opportunity of hearing the truth from His lips. He kneeled before Him, beseeching Him to instruct him; he addressed Him with open reverence and admiration, and put to Him the most solemn of all questions, as to how he might be safe and happy and holy for eternity. So open and ingenuous was he, so truthful as far as his light extended in his reply to our Lord's address, as to win a token of approval from the gentle Saviour. 'Jesus beholding him loved him;' that is to say, as the original implies, He cast a loving look upon him. At first that look seems to have had no effect upon him; he loved his riches more than his soul's welfare. It may be that in after days the memory of that look had power to bring him back to God, but of this we cannot be certain. He came to Christ confident of his own ability to save himself, evidently supposing that little, if anything, was wanting in a man of such excellent moral character as he conceived himself to be, in order to secure an entrance into life eternal. Our Lord takes him at his own estimate; He does not stay to point out to him the defects in his obedience to the second table of the law. He shows him that even *had* he observed all its commands, as he said, from his youth, there was a duty owing to God of equal obligation, of primary importance. He lays upon him a command which would test and prove the state of his heart towards God: 'Go thy way, sell whatsoever thou hast, and give to the poor, and thou shalt have treasure in heaven, and come, take up the cross, and follow Me.'

Poor rich man! by his conduct he showed that he could not save self by his works, and that he was not willing to surrender self to Christ, who could save him by His grace. 'He was sad at that saying, and went away grieved, for he had great possessions.' How great the difference between his behaviour and that of another man who doubtless was, to some extent, also rich—Levi or Matthew the publican, who at the Saviour's call made no excuse, sought no delay, but 'left all, rose up, and followed Him.' How different, too, the conduct of those poor fishers of the Galilean lake, who at the voice of Jesus brought their little vessels to the shore, forsook all, and followed Him.

The condition set before us in these words of our Lord is that of a man in whom, as we say, 'there is a great deal that is good,' but who *lacks one thing*. And remember always, brethren, that it is an *intentional* lacking, a *wilful* keeping back of something which God demands from us, and we withhold from Him that is so dangerous, so fatal. This young man was seeking salvation earnestly, humbly, in an upright, chaste, kind, and dutiful way of life—so amiable, so lovely, as to win a glance of affection from the Saviour; but he could not, and would not, surrender his wealth to God. One thing wanting, and we know not that this deficiency was ever supplied. There is a somewhat similar case in St. Mark, xii. 28–34, the case of a scribe who had an intelligent appreciation of the great truths of religion so far as they were then fully revealed. He cheerfully approved them, he publicly owned their excellence, he bore testimony to those truths, unpopular as they were, publicly, honestly, fearlessly; he perceived the true principle of obedience, love to God and man; he owned that without this love or charity all outward observance of religion was vain and worthless. He was pronounced by Christ to be not far from the kingdom of God,—*not far*, but we know not that he ever entered in.

Look at a third instance, that of King Agrippa, in Acts, xxvi. 28—a man in a high worldly position, surrounded by temptation. He hears the cause of the gospel pleaded by a prisoner in chains, despised and persecuted. He boldly avows his admiration of it, and in the presence of envious Jews and sneering heathen owns himself almost persuaded to embrace it. *Almost*, yet it is to be feared never quite, never *altogether* persuaded. The Bible account leaves all of these unconverted, *not* saved, in a state of condemnation. One thing in each case, and probably *only* one, stood between the man and his God, between the sinner and salvation. In the first instance worldliness, in the second self-righteous pride, in the third sensuality and unlawful love. One thing, it may be only one, but that one enough to ruin each soul.

My brethren, in whom so much that is good, so much that is amiable, so much religiousness is found, who do so many things for God's sake and hear the gospel gladly, look to it that there be not in any of you this deficiency that ruins the soul, this one thing that keeps man back from God. In these three instances which I have just enumerated the one thing lacking, the real deficiency, was the same, though the outward sign of the deficiency was in each case different. The one thing lacking was the disposition to surrender *self* to God, to give up to Him body, soul, and spirit, rank and property, passions and prejudices, to be dealt with and corrected at His will—the disposition to accept salvation on His terms, and to govern the life by His laws. This is the one thing needful that these men had not. Levi the publican had it, the woman that had been a sinner had it, the thief on the cross had it, and they were saved.

My brethren, if we have any reserve from God, anything that we are wilfully keeping back from Him, not merely any outward possession, not merely any act of outward obedience, but any prejudice of the mind, any thought or affection of the heart which we refuse to submit to His will, we are not loyal subjects of the kingdom of heaven; we are not saved or reconciled to God. I dread that word '*but*' in religion; I dread to hear it from the lips of *man*, because God demands *all*. Not that He bids us give up all, but He will have us *ready* to give up all, should He call for the surrender. Our Lord has said, 'If any man come after Me, and hate not his father, and mother, and wife, and children, and brothers, and sisters, yea, and his own life also, he cannot be My disciple.' (St. Luke, xiv. 26.) And the meaning of that word 'hate' is best explained by the example of a presbyter of our own Church. This man was led to the fire, there to die for the truth of the Lord. As he passed along the streets of London he was met by his wife and little children, who came to say farewell to the husband and the father. At that hour of trial he had but to give his outward assent to those errors of the Church of Rome that destroy the soul, and his life would have been spared, and he himself restored to those whom he loved so well. But he gave up all for Christ, and took up his cross and followed his Saviour. He went on cheerfully to his death, and through the fire passed to his Lord. He had *the one thing* (the readiness to surrender all *for* and *to* God).

My brethren, who profess to be religious people, let us ask ourselves, Is the one thing lacking in *us?* One sin, one guilty compliance, one inconsistency, knowingly and wilfully persisted in, one evil habit, one sinful affection, one wrong pleasure or amusement which we do not try to conquer or resign, one possession, one treasure which we would not give up, if called so to do for Christ's sake,—any of these is the sign that the *one thing* is lacking in us,—any of these is a barrier between us and our God,—any of these shuts us out from God's kingdom of grace here, and will banish us from His kingdom of glory hereafter for ever.

The condition of this man in our text was most dangerous ; he was in the greater danger because he seemed so near to safety. *One thing lacking—only one;* and so with the others whose history I have referred to. 'Not far from the kingdom of God;' 'Almost persuaded to be a Christian.' How many in such case say to themselves, We are all but safe ; we need not be, as others, alarmed about our condition ; we stand at mercy's open gate, and whenever we choose to lay aside the *one* hindrance we can enter in. And so they stand secure ; they see the prodigal from a far country come up and bathe in the blood of cleansing, and clothe himself in the white robe of Christ's righteousness, and go in at the gate. They are so near that they can almost hear the angelic strains that welcome each repentant sinner. In all this they find pleasure and contentment, for, say they, soon we too will enter there ; such a welcome also awaits *us*. But an hour comes when the door is shut. Just as they imagined, perhaps, that they would enter, they are shut out for ever.

My brethren, let us pray God that we be not

self-deceivers in this. Where there is but *one thing* lacking we may fancy that all is well; and let us carefully and with prayer ask ourselves, Have we any reserve from God? Are we afraid to look too narrowly into our hearts and lives, lest we discover some one thing wrong which we do not wish to have set right? Let us not rest till we can say, 'I count *all* things but loss for the excellency of the knowledge of Christ Jesus my Lord.' (Phil. iii. 8.)

Nor think, my brethren, that in our Master's name we ask too much. We ask you for complete self-surrender, but it is for His sake who gave up all for you, and took thorns for His crown and the cross for His throne, and bare all the burden and the guilt and punishment of our sins; Himself overcoming the sharpness of death and opening the kingdom of heaven to all believers, that the very chief of sinners who would come and ask Him might be saved, and numbered with His saints in glory everlasting.

## V.

### FAITHFULNESS OVER FEW TALENTS.

St. Matthew, xxv., part of ver. 23.—'Faithful over a few things.'

WE must not confound the parable from which our text is taken, the Parable of the Talents, with that of the Pounds as recorded by St. Luke. The first was spoken to the disciples, and spoken at Jerusalem; the other probably at Jericho, and delivered to the multitudes. They are two distinct parables, or rather two distinct editions of the same parable, adapted to two distinct classes of hearers, and intended to convey somewhat different lessons.

I desire to-day to call your attention, not to the general scope of the parable of the talents, but rather to some special points in its teaching suggested by the words of the text. Learn by contrast the sin of,

I. Unfaithfulness over a few things, of neglecting to work for God and in the service of His Church on earth, because few talents (it may be only one) are intrusted to your care. Thereby you lose 'Well done,' and gain the sentence (in ver. 30), ' Cast ye the unprofitable servant into outer darkness : there shall be weeping and gnashing of teeth.' This sin springs from various causes ; most frequently from unbelief. The servant in the parable did not believe in the kindness and justice of his Lord : ' My master requires so much, and gives so little, that it is vain for me to try to please him.' The whole Bible shows the falsehood of this excuse. How great the rewards bestowed on, and the promises held out to, such as doing little yet do what they can to serve God and show love to His dear Son. Remember the barrel of meal and cruse of oil ; the rope of Ebed-melech so kindly covered lest it should hurt the prophet's emaciated frame as he was drawn up out of the dungeon ; the cup of cold water ; the two mites. One there was who had nothing ; she could offer but tears of penitence and love wherewith to bathe the Redeemer's feet ; she hears the announcement of her pardon forthwith. Another anoints with essence those feet so soon to be nailed to the cross for her, and is repaid by the highest form of praise : ' She hath done what she could.'

Moreover, this sin of unfaithfulness in the use of talents arises, says our Lord, from *slothfulness*. Such servants are lovers of pleasure more than lovers of God; glad of the excuse 'talents few' as a plea for giving themselves up to self-gratification, as if those talents were their own of right, and not a loan intrusted to their charge. And yet another cause of this sin is *pride*. Says the unprofitable servant, Why have others more talents than I? Am I not as deserving? Why is my station less influential than theirs? Why can I do nothing worthy of myself—nothing in comparison with the successes achieved by them? I will, then, attempt nothing, lest what I do should not win for me the praise and credit without which I cannot be contented. One and the same doom is pronounced on all who act in the spirit of such excuses: 'Cast ye the unprofitable servant into outer darkness.'

Notice, II. He who has most talents is, after all, intrusted with but few, while on earth, in comparison with the talents and opportunities for serving and glorifying God that will be given to the redeemed in heaven; but few compared with those which the angels enjoy. He cannot excel in strength like them, roaming the universe, flying very swiftly to do His pleasure. He is shut up within the limits of earth, generally of a small corner of earth, tied and bound by the weakness and sinfulness of fallen nature, and of mortal capacity. Even he to whom most talents were intrusted is spoken of as faithful over a *few* things, and some of us have fewer talents than others, some only two, others five. God, who gives to each man his ability, gives talents to each according to that ability. One is crippled in his exertions in God's service by poverty, another by ignorance, another by weak health. Old age, disappointment, solitude, and the like, all hinder us in holy work; and these things are best known to our Lord. Who, with talents for doing good as with all else, divideth to every man severally as He will. Let no man, then, be disposed to boast himself in the number or to despair at the fewness of the talents committed to his care for service. Of the greatest and of the least allotment our Lord speaks, as being alike but 'few things;' yet consider—

III. That the talents entrusted to each man's care, though 'few things,' and even fewer to some than others, are nowhere mentioned lightly, or spoken of as *little* things. Each Christian man is endowed with great things, by which he may serve and honour his God. He who has the knowledge of his Maker, Redeemer, Sanctifier, who doth in his soul feel and know that Christ is his salvation. He who can read the Bible, he who cannot read it, but to whom God has given ears to hear it, and memory to store passages in his mind, hath lent unto him by God talents *great*, if few. Who is there who, if he has the grace of the Holy Ghost in his heart, may not be the means of *saving one soul*, leading one erring one to the cross of Christ, adding one jewel, it may be, yet at least one, to the crown of Him who died for us?

Moreover, if the angels have more talents intrusted to them than we, some talents are lent us that they have never known. Rich and happy, untempted, immortal, they cannot glorify God as he can who is gifted with grace to serve in weakness, weariness, and woe. Nay, the Christian on earth hath talents which even the redeemed in glory have not. You may stand by the bedside of some sufferer in a workhouse ward, whose calm, pain-stricken face, and trusting patience are by grace ever offering praise to God, that thrills the hearts of angel-watchers and speaks piercingly to fellow-sinners. It proclaims to all a Father's goodness, and tells of the love of Christ, and of the power of the Comforter; and Heaven itself cannot witness praise like that except as a memory of conflict over and victory won. And to turn to every-day life. A Christian of, it may be, very poor mental capacity, placed in no circumstances of unusual trial, stirred up to serve by no duties of an exciting kind, can most highly exalt the glory of his God in the eyes of witnesses far more numerous than he knows. This by simple obedience to the word of God in common duties and by patient continuance in well-doing. Let no man complain that his talents are *few;* none of us have many,—all have great talents, opportunities for glorifying God and winning, not earning, from a Saviour's lips that crown of praise—' Good and faithful servant ; thou hast been faithful over a few things.'

Consider next what is required of God's servants—

IV. Fidelity. The servant in the text is not praised for his success, but for his *faithfulness.* It is not in man's power, even though he be earnest, and conscientious, and prayerful, to ensure outward success in his efforts to use his talents to the glory of God. But be those talents many or few, faithfulness in the use of them is that which God looks for, and which God is pleased to approve. What, then, is this fidelity ? It is a gift of the Holy Ghost, bestowed on us as a mercy. So St. Paul speaks of his own faithfulness (1 Cor. xv. 10) : ' But by the grace of God I am what I am ; and His grace, which was bestowed upon me, was not in vain ; but I laboured more abundantly than they all; yet not I, but the grace of God which was with me.' It is to be sought in earnest prayer, and in common with other necessary gifts of the Holy Ghost; it is promised in answer to such prayer, offered in the name of the Lord Jesus Christ.

Faithfulness, then, includes in it the simple belief and the continual remembrance that all our powers, possessions, and opportunities, are lent to us by God, and are His and not our own; talents entrusted to our use with this charge: 'Occupy till I come;' nay more, that we ourselves are not our own, but bought with a price, and therefore bound to glorify God with our bodies and our spirits, which are His.* Bearing this in mind, the faithful man is one who earnestly sets to work to find out what talents he has in his charge, and to use them as in his Master's sight for purposes for which they appear to have been bestowed by God. He will not murmur at the talents assigned him, because they are not such as he would have chosen, nor will he be discontented at the opportunities afforded him of using those talents, be they many or few. If his talents be such as to bring him earthly praise and reputation, he will pray for humility, and should they be such as to attract no human notice or applause, he will strive by grace to be thankful. Such an one would esteem himself unfaithful indeed did he not persevere in his efforts, did he suffer himself

* Our Lord in the parable uses the word δοῦλος.

to relax them because of the want of immediate success, or to be turned from the right path by the temptations of the Evil One. Popularity or unpopularity affect him not; those words, 'Who loved me and gave Himself for me,' are ever present to his mind, as the first principles of his life's work. And these are seconded by those other words, 'Christ in you *the hope of glory.*' His rule in all things is 'to the Lord and not unto men;' and his privilege is to feel with St. Paul, 'To me to live is Christ, and to die is gain.' How far we fall short of this standard is known and felt by every Christian soul. May we be awakened by thus contemplating it to greater diligence in using the talents committed to our care.

Glance, in conclusion, at—

V. The reward. We are in all our attempts to serve and glorify our God to be both stimulated and encouraged by the thought that He who died for us is looking on, watching us with tender love, and—with reverence be it spoken—as He sees our poor efforts made for His sake, experiencing that Divine satisfaction which was promised Him by the Father in Isaiah (liii. 11): 'He shall see of the travail of His soul, and shall be satisfied.' The *thought* alone of this is reward, far more than enough, for all that we can do.

But the text carries us on to the opening of

the books and the Lord's recognition of His servants. His coming to take them home ; His bestowing on them the reward of eternal glory, earned by Him, but which He rejoices to make theirs. And it leads us to the throne, to hear from the very lips once so parched with dying thirst for us at Calvary : ' Well done, good and faithful servant ; enter thou into the joy of thy Lord.' (St. Matt. xxv. 23.)

## VI.

#### THE SIGHTS IN THE HOUSE.

ISA. xxxix., part of verse 4.—'What have they seen in thine house?'

WERE certain strangers, brethren, to come among us to-day and to form their estimate of our character and pursuits from such of our actions as are publicly visible, were they to judge of us from our behaviour here, from the words of our prayers, and the songs of praise that proceed from our lips, it is probable their opinion of us might be favourable: that they would say, surely God is among these people, and His Spirit dwells within them. This seems at first sight to be reasonable. From what source, it might be asked, should any one judge of our state before God, if not from our demeanour on His day, and in our gathering together in His presence. *Very true*, were there but one command, 'Keep My Sabbaths, and reverence My Sanctuary.' *Very reasonable*, were we not bidden to take the word of God as our rule when we *walk* by the *way*, as well as when we join in the hallowed duties of the day of rest, and take part in the sacred rites of the house of prayer. Let these imaginary strangers, then, be admitted to further intimacy with us; let them meet us on the Monday morning, and accompany us through the remainder of the week. In the places of our daily employments and pleasures—the field, the desk, the shop—let them enter into business relations and social intercourse with us; would not their estimate of the amount of true religion among us be greatly lowered? Would they not be obliged to confess that they had been mistaken, and that the number of servants of God among us was far smaller than they had supposed? That too many of us were, after all, but Sunday Christians; and *yet* they would find, I think, not a few who were so honest and true in their dealings, so kind and gentle in manner, so far from any impropriety of behaviour—who had God and His service so often upon their lips—that they would still think well of us upon the whole. They would rejoice, that though there were many of us whose religion came on by weekly fits, and lasted them only the seventh part of their time, yet that many must indeed be real Christians, since they carried their religion into their daily employments, and put honour upon God's law, in their public intercourse with the world. But

## THE SIGHTS IN THE HOUSE. 55

even so they would not be justified in their opinion. Religion claims a great deal more than this. The law of God is given us to be taught to our families, by precept and example; we are to make it our guide when we sit in the house as well as when we worship in the sanctuary, or walk by the way of more public life. It is to be the rule of our thoughts, and words, and actions, when we lie down, and when we rise up, to regulate our most private as well as our public life. Whatsoever we do we are to do all to the glory of God. Let us, then, ask ourselves, what kind of character we should obtain if our life and conduct were to be judged by such a standard as this: if we and our religion were to be estimated by the *sights to be seen in our homes*.

If we turn to the passage before us we shall see that, when the ambassadors of the King of Babylon came to King Hezekiah, he showed them all his treasures—gold, and spices, and precious ointment, and all the house of his armour—there was nothing in his house nor in all his dominion that Hezekiah showed them not. Doubtless there was much to show. There would be all the spoil of the Assyrian army, so terribly destroyed near Jerusalem when it was returning to Nineveh, laden with the plunder of conquered countries. They saw much to convince them of Hezekiah's greatness, but they seem to have seen nothing to lead them to Hezekiah's God. They probably went home, having seen nothing of Hezekiah's real piety, of his gratitude for recovery from sickness, little or nothing that could glorify God, or tend to make them better and wiser men. Then comes the Prophet with the solemn question, 'What have they seen in thine house?' Let us apply this question to ourselves, and let the words remind us, brethren, first of this truth,—

I. The Christian is watched—watched as to the conduct of his private and family life. I do not now refer to the unsleeping vigilance of the eye of Almighty God, but to the observation of created beings. By them there is a degree of watchfulness exercised, far beyond all that we are disposed to imagine. Angels watch us; as ministering spirits they are conversant with the affairs of men to a very great extent, employed by God to attend His people, to oppose and counteract on their behalf the designs of evil men and evil spirits; it is impossible but that we should be surrounded by these messengers of heaven. This fact appears very plainly from Holy Scripture, where we find that, on several occasions, when the eyes of the beholder were miraculously opened, the angels were distinctly seen as they performed their appointed offices. Again Devils watch us. Though fallen spirits, yet like the angels they, too, are spirits; no walls, no doors can shut them out. They pervade the very air we breathe, under their chief, the Prince of the power of the air: they are ever roaming about, watching for means of temptation, for opportunities of evil, seeking whom they may devour. Then, also, *Men* watch us, especially if, like Hezekiah, we profess to be religious people. How important the question which we consider secondly,—

II. 'What have they seen in thine house?' Do they see God or the world ruling there? which is best served? which is the real master? Do they behold in a wealthy house a lavish expenditure on the things of time which is denied to those of eternity? Whilst thou, O Christian, dost plead inability to do more for the service of God, for the education of children in the fear of God, for Christian missions, for the feeding the hungry and clothing the naked, what have the watchers seen in thine house? Silver and gold laid up to thine own hurt; expensive furniture which must come down at last to one narrow bier; costly entertainments to pamper the bodies that will soon be a feast for worms; money laid out on dress that is denied to Christ. Poor man! 'what have they seen in thine house?' Disorder, negligence, and uncleanness; indulgence in gross and carnal pleasures, little fitting those who hope to be companions of angels? Master or mistress, 'what have they seen in thine house?' The day begun with God? Some time set apart in which all the members of the family meet in the morning to give thanks for the rest and safety of the night, and to seek pardon for each sinful thought, and to beseech God's presence with them through the day? Is this the morning voice heard in thy house?

> 'Wake and lift up thyself, my heart,
> And with the angels bear thy part:
> Who all night long unwearied sing
> High glory to the Eternal King.'

Are all the inmates of the house and the stranger that is within thy gates seen to join in prayer at the close of day, lifting up their hands as an acceptable evening sacrifice? Is religion seen to be the ruling principle in your house? When the service of God comes in contact with household affairs, which gives way? Is family prayer put aside for the sake of company? Is your care for those whom you employ confined to giving them the opportunity of going to church, or do they find that you really seek their souls, and that you take pains to instruct and guide them in the way they should go by precept and by example? Parents, what do your children see in your houses? Do they see you commit offences which you teach *them* to avoid? Do they see you make light of sin against God while you punish severely any sin against yourselves? Do they see that the opinion of the world has more weight with you than the command of God? Do they see the Bible read and reverenced by you? Have they been taught to live soberly, industriously, and orderly in the fear of God, and in obedience to the sovereign, and to such as are in authority under her, by seeing that *you* try so to live? Or are the lessons of the Bible, of the School, and of the Church, rendered unavailing by your inconsistent and evil example? Children, what do others see of *your* behaviour in the house? Obedience to your parents, industry in such work as they have a right to expect from you, love to one another and to them, truth and honesty in word and deed? Or do they see your fathers and mothers made miserable by your ungodliness and disobedience, your home profaned by quarrelling and strife, yourselves a burden to those to whom God sent you to be a blessing? Professing Christian people, what do the watchers see in *your* homes? An earnest endeavour to bring all things into subjection to the law of God, Christian tempers, Christian conversation, Christian practices? Or are those tempers and that language kept for home, which you are afraid or ashamed to manifest or to use abroad? Are disorder and misrule, strife and envy, and every evil work, to be seen there, while outside its walls you are patterns of decency and propriety? Did time permit, these questions might be extended to a far greater length; but, so far as they go, they are questions of weighty consequence.

. III. Consider their *importance* as regards yourselves and others. Your household conduct and character afford a pretty sure indication of *your own* spiritual state. If God be served and reverenced in the house, where the motives to that unconscious hypocrisy which is so common, are neither as many nor as strong as in our more public life, *then* is there a good hope that He is feared and loved in the heart. If, on the contrary, you disregard Him at home, if He does not rule your conduct there, then all your public sayings and doings, all your out-of-doors religion is little worth; indeed it is very offensive to Him, who looks closer even than the home, for He looks at the heart. Again, the practical answer to these questions afforded by our conduct is of infinite importance as to its effect upon *others*. It takes effect in places where we might fancy that it was not known or noticed. In the home of a consistent Christian are sights to be seen that add to the glory of God, and increase the pleasures of heaven. Angels, who have joy over one sinner that repents, do not surely think it beneath them to rejoice over the godly household of a godly family—over one consistent servant of their Master even in an irreligious home. And there are sights to be seen, and sounds to be heard in the family of a mere nominal Christian that form matter of hateful triumph to the very devils. These are glad at the prospect of obtaining fresh victims for their malice. They rejoice in the injury done to the souls for whom the Saviour died. Further, the sights in the house are important in their effect upon our brethren. Not only may servants, lodgers, children, friends, be led, through grace, by your holy example in home privacy, to value the religion that produces such fruits, and to accept your Saviour for themselves; but be sure, brethren, that more is known abroad of your behaviour at home, and of the things to be seen in your homes, than you suppose. By these things men judge, not only of you—*that* were of small importance— but by these things men are very ready to form their opinion of your religion and of your Lord. They know that many motives of an earthly kind may induce you to *profess* godliness, and to observe an outward propriety of demeanour. If they find that your religion leads you no further, that it has no effect upon your private conduct, they will come to suppose that it is nothing more than worldly prudence. Earthly wisdom, with the addition of a little hypocrisy, and that all its professed power over the man is but vain and empty boasting. On the other hand, let them find that when you do not know you are observed you act as if the eyes of all were upon you. Let them find that godliness brings peace to your firesides, that actions at home agree with profession abroad, that it is *God's* praise and not theirs for which you are looking. Then is there hope that they will be led to admire the religion that produces such results, to acknowledge its excellence, to believe its truth, and, if God be pleased to give His Holy Spirit, men may be brought to desire to know more of Him whose name you bear, and be, by your example, not only almost but altogether persuaded to be Christians.

Finally, brethren, let me remind you of the agency of the Holy Ghost in this matter. If the sights seen in your homes are to be such as are edifying to your families and neighbours, such as are good for yourselves, and conducive to the glory of God, it can only be through the abiding presence of the Divine Spirit in your hearts. Ask Him to be in you, a spirit of prayer. All the efforts of many well-meaning persons fail, because while they try to do much they pray coldly or indifferently, or without reliance on God's answers to prayer. Remember the blessing on the household and friends of Cornelius. Herein lay the secret of his success in winning it for them and for himself: 'He prayed to God alway,' (Acts, x. 2.) May that spirit be in us, brethren, a spirit of wisdom, and discretion, and love, as well as of earnestness and zeal. Let your constraining motive in all this be the love of Christ—the remembrance that He died to save *all* that will come to Him—the memory of His passion. A disorderly and ill-governed family, especially when it is that of a professing Christian, is very grievous in your Saviour's sight. But a peaceful and godly household is His delight. 'Behold, saith the Lord, how good and pleasant a thing it is for brethren to dwell together in unity,' (Ps. cxxxiii.) What reason does God assign for His familiar converse with Abraham whom He honoured with the title of His friend? and for the blessings promised to him? (Gen. xviii. 19.) 'For I know him, that he will command his children and his household after him, and they shall keep the way of the Lord, to do justice and judgment; that the Lord may bring upon Abraham that which He hath spoken of him.'

Parents and masters, in this duty of a well-ordered and pious *home*, I cannot point you to the example of the Lord our Saviour. House of His own He never possessed; many a time while the foxes had holes, and the birds of the air their nests, the Son of man had not where to lay His head.

Sons, and daughters, and servants, if you sometimes find the strict rules of a Christian home irksome and inconvenient, if they ever seem to hinder your innocent pleasures, and to interfere with your independence, remember that God's own Son, who loved *you*, when He was old enough to reason with and examine the teachers of religion in the Temple, at the desire of His mother and her husband went down with them to their poor home at Nazareth, and was 'subject unto them.'

## VII.

### THE PRESENCE OF OUR LORD AT UNITED WORSHIP.

St. Matt. xviii., part of verse 20.—'There am I.'

SUCH is the influence of Christians with Christ, such the power of united prayer! Before entering on the consideration of the text, let me call your attention to a very important lesson which it teaches by the way. And that is, never to make light of any assembly gathered in the name of the Lord Jesus. Such assemblies may consist of unlearned and ignorant men, and their language may sound harsh and uncouth in the ears of the educated and refined. To us who are members of a Church so apostolic in discipline, and so Scriptural in doctrine, the notions held by others as to ecclesiastical constitution and government may appear deficient or erroneous. Their Master is in these, as in all other matters, their Judge. But if they be true Christians, their voice hath in it a charm to call down the King of Kings from heaven, and in the midst of them there is He!

Let us consider first the person of the speaker:

F

I. 'There am I.' He who stood and spake thus was, to the eye of the hearers, a very poor, sorrowful, and despised man. Nor did He only *appear* so; such as He *appeared*, He most truly *was*. Once a little child, then a toiling man, then a teacher, living as other men lived; hungering and thirsting, weary and needing rest; at length bowing His head in death, and borne a lifeless corpse to His burial. By loving hands wound in grave-clothes, and laid in a sepulchre; full of all sinless human feelings, of all most tender human sympathies; son, brother, friend, perfect man, of a reasonable soul, and human flesh subsisting. How could these things be? How could this man keep a promise that only God could perform? There is but one answer to the question. The speaker was God, the eternal Word, the only begotten Son, of one substance with the Father. The awful Jehovah Himself, Whom heaven, and the heaven of heavens, cannot contain. The words of our text are a direct assertion of His Godhead. 'There am I!' Who else could say so? Who else could offer his presence, wheresoever any two or three of his servants should meet in his name? The unlimited offer of the Infinite God. How can these things be? I know not, I cannot explain the mystery; angels cannot fathom it, eternity will not unfold it.

Yet I believe, I am assured, that the speaker was both God and man. On that truth I rest. On that truth are built all my hopes for time and for eternity. God and man, yet not two, but one Christ. He soon proved the truth of His claim. Laid in the tomb as man, the tomb with the very great stone rolled to the door, sealed and watched. As God, He passes through all these vain attempts to keep Him in the prison-house of death. The angels roll away the stone, but the body of the crucified is not there. He hath already risen; behold the place where the Lord lay. The Lord, 'declared to be the Son of God with power, by the resurrection from the dead.' The sun hath not clearly risen on His resurrection ere He begins to keep the promise in the text. Two women are going to tell His disciples of the empty tomb, and on the way there is He! Jesus met them, 'saying All hail!' Two disciples on a journey that evening, speak of His name. There is He! 'Jesus Himself drew near and went with them.' He leaves them at Emmaus, and at once they rise and hasten back to Jerusalem; eager and breathless they tell their glorious news, and, lo, as they speak, there is He! 'Jesus Himself stood in the midst of them.' This is He by whom my text was spoken. The same yesterday, and to-day, and for ever, able and willing to-day just as on that first glorious Easter to keep the promise, and where two or three are gathered in His name, there to be in the midst of them. What presence so suited to the wants of them that meet to worship God? Two or three sinful creatures gathered in the sight of Him that is of purer eyes than to behold iniquity. Such this assembly of ours to-day, so far as man sees it. God sees more; *One* more! In the midst of us, a Lamb as it had been slain. And for the sake of that sacrifice He hath cast all our sins behind His back. Two or three weak and helpless ones who desire to be holy, and would fain be made fit to dwell in the presence of their holy Creator for ever. Unseen, yet in the midst of us most truly is the Giver of the Spirit of holiness the Holy Ghost. Two or three, full of human affections, with all the pains and pleasures, the hopes and fears, that those affections bring with them, and in the midst He in whose human heart all sinless human affections dwelt with a force and earnestness beyond our power to imagine. Two or three; yet I fear some lost wanderers among us, but in the midst of us One who is come to seek and save the lost. Two or three dying people, and in the midst the Conqueror of death, the Spoiler of the grave. Lord! we believe that Thou art here; help Thou our unbelief. As of old make our hearts to burn within us, as by Thy Spirit Thou dost speak with us by the way, and open to us the Scriptures.

Consider next: II. Where this speaker is to be found,—the answer to the longing desire of Job, 'Oh that I knew where I might find Him, that I might come even to His seat' (Job, xxiii. 3),—the answer to the universal cry of the whole creation after the Creator, whose face was withdrawn at the fall. A sinful, suffering, dying world stretches forth her hands to feel after and find a God who can and will give pardon and happiness and endless life. How blessed the Lord's voice in reply, 'Where two or three are gathered together in My name, there am I in the midst of them.' We need no ceremonial pomp to win the favouring presence of our Lord; no toilsome pilgrimage to seek His face: where two or three are gathered in each home, where the inmates join in prayer and praise; though it may be that the home is poor, and the inhabitants but two, there is He! No palace high enough for His glory, no cottage too mean for His love. In each Christian school, and, above all, in every house of prayer, He is to be found. You cannot miss His presence, brethren, if only two come together in the hope of meeting Him. You can bring the King of Kings in most loving, sympathising presence into your company when and where any two of you agree to call Him down. There is no place on earth which may not be made by any two Christian people to be the very house of God, the very gate of heaven. But this blessing has its limitations, or rather there are conditions annexed to it. The two or three gathered together must be assembled in the name of Christ. It may to some appear to be an uncharitable interpretation, but I feel assured that it is the *true* one, which limits the promise to such as hold right doctrine as far as their light extends concerning the Lord Jesus Christ; to those who recognise the truth to which I have already alluded in the first part of my subject. The expression the 'name' of Christ is used in Holy Scripture to signify far more than the mere appellative by which He is called. It comprehends the fulness of His nature, His attributes, and all that glorious office of Mediator which brought Him down on earth, and which He now fulfils in heaven at the right hand of God the Father. In these days men too often set up as the object of their faith and trust some imaginary person whom they dignify with the name of Christ. As of old some said that He was John the Baptist, and some Elias, and others Jeremias. So now some cry *Ecce Homo*, and leave out of sight His Godhead. And some point to Him as one who came to prove the love of God to man, and deny that He came to be wounded for our transgressions, and bruised for our iniquities, and to put away sin by the sacrifice of Himself. My brethren, the promise is made by Him who said, 'I and my Father are One;' 'Before Abraham was I am.' By Him who was made sin for us, and who bore our curse upon the Cross. The promise is made to them, and to them alone, that gather in His name; in the name that characterises Him as He is; to them that accept Him in the twofold nature that is ascribed to Him in Holy Scripture as the God-Man, their Prophet, Priest, and King. If we would have this promised presence among us, it is necessary that we believe rightly the incarnation of our Lord Jesus Christ. For the right faith is, that we believe and confess that our Lord Jesus Christ, the Son of God, is God and man; Who suffered for our salvation, descended into hell; the third day He rose again from the dead. He ascended into heaven. He sitteth on the right hand of the Father, God Almighty; from whence He shall come to judge the quick and the dead.

Look to,—III. The purpose of His presence. It appears from verse 19 that He comes especially to hear the prayers of His people, and to offer them with acceptance to His Father. 'Again I say unto you, that if two of you shall agree on earth as touching anything that they shall ask, it shall be done for them of My Father, which is in heaven.'

This consideration should lead us to ask ourselves, Why did we come together this day? The Lord is present, Who sees our hearts. Does He see amidst much wandering and imperfection that we came to meet *Him*, to tell Him our need of pardon and grace, our earthly wants, our spiritual necessities, to pray for others as well as for ourselves? In the prayers to-day has there been the *agreement* He speaks of, or have we been outwardly gathered together, yet in spirit unmindful of each other's presence, and each other's need: praying 'Our Father,' yet meaning my Father, praying 'Give us,' yet meaning Give me; crying 'We beseech Thee,' while we meant 'I beseech Thee.' This is not the prayer of two agreeing to which the special promise is annexed.

In order that we may realise the fulfilment of this promise, we must ask of God unity of spirit, grace to pray the Church's prayers. This should be the spirit of our petitions, ' *We* beseech Thee to hear *us*, Good Lord.' The promise in the text, 'There am I,' is but one among many tokens of our Lord's desire for unity among His people, ' that they may be one as We are,' according to His prayer, St. John, xvii. 11. What an opportunity is afforded us in the assemblies of

Christians of winning an inestimable blessing for ourselves, each other, the Church, and the world! Here is *Christ* in the midst of us, Christ in whom dwelleth all the fulness of the Godhead, of whose fulness all we may receive—'Ask and ye shall receive, that your joy may be full.' Brethren, 'Let *us* pray.'

In our text we have a warning to those who say, Why should we frequent the house of prayer; we can pray as well at home? Surely, brethren, the place of which our Lord says, 'There am I,' is the best place for you. Not on the Lord's day alone, but whensoever Christian people gather together in His name. If Christian men could but enter into the spirit of these words, we should not have to lament over the scant attendance at the week-day services of our Church. It is sad that when our Saviour says, 'There am I,' it should be true of any of His servants, as of St. Thomas, 'He was not with them when Jesus came!' And you, O baptized, unconverted; you who are here to-day for any other purpose than to meet your Lord, your Saviour who died to win you; you who come from mere habit or custom, as a matter of respectability; you who do not really care for Christ, yet who believe that He shall come to be your judge,—what shall I say to you? Think on those words, 'There am I.' At this moment your loving Lord is *here*. You may never meet Him again till you see Him on the great white throne. Full of love waiting to bless you, your Lord is here now. 'There standeth One among you whom ye know not.'

## VIII.

### CHRIST THE FOOD OF THE SOUL.
### FOR THE HOLY COMMUNION.

St. JOHN, vi. 53-55. — 'Then Jesus said unto them, Verily, verily, I say unto you, Except ye eat the flesh of the Son of man, and drink His blood, ye have no life in you. Whoso eateth My flesh, and drinketh My blood, hath eternal life; and I will raise him up at the last day. For My flesh is meat indeed, and My blood is drink indeed.'

MAN, naturally blind to the things of the Spirit, thinks nothing real but that which is perceptible by the bodily senses. Hence the attempts from the days of our Lord's sojourn on earth till now to put a carnal sense on these words. As did the Jews (ver. 52): 'The Jews therefore strove among themselves, saying, How can this man give us His flesh to eat?' And the Romanists do so by applying this text to the bread and wine in the Holy Communion. Now, no literal bodily feeding on Christ is possible. Christ, when these words were spoken, was alive in body, and is now alive at the right hand of

God in bodily presence; and the body of Christ, a human body, cannot be in two places at once, *there* and also between the lips of His people. Nor is feeding on Christ confined to the hour of the Lord's Supper, for when Christ spoke the text the Lord's Supper was not instituted. It is a spiritual food that is here intended (ver. 63): 'It is the spirit that quickeneth; the flesh profiteth nothing: the words that I speak unto you, they are spirit, and they are life.' And the Christian feeds on Christ by faith (ver. 47): 'He that believeth on Me hath everlasting life.' I would direct your attention to—

I. The statement, 'My flesh is meat *indeed*, and My blood is drink *indeed*.' Here a comparison is instituted between our Lord Jesus and earthly food, but by that emphatic *truly* or *indeed* our Lord seems to intimate that even in an earthly sense the sign falls short of the thing signified, as indeed it does. The things which we eat and drink serve for three purposes—for healing, for support, for pleasure. The body and blood of the Lord not only do cure and sustain and delight the living soul, but they buy life for the soul under sentence of death eternal; they give life to the lifeless soul. For a world under sentence of eternal death Christ gave Himself to die, the just for the unjust, by travail of soul *atoning*, and this through the Father's love : 'The Lord hath laid on Him the iniquity of us all.' 'God so loved the world, that He gave His only-begotten Son, that whosoever believeth on Him should not perish, but have everlasting life.' By His precious blood-shedding He made a full, perfect, and sufficient sacrifice, oblation, and satisfaction for the sins of the whole world. Thus (ver. 51) : 'The bread that I will give is My flesh, which I will give for the life of the world.'

Moreover, it is Christ's body and blood that give life to the lifeless soul. The soul is by nature without one feeling, one desire, one affection, as it ought to be. Without any feeling towards God but dislike of His holy law, an uneasy sense of His presence, and dread of His future vengeance. By the application of this life-giving food to it by the Holy Ghost the soul is not only shown the beauty of holiness in the life and death of Christ, the love of God in Christ, and the hope of peace with the prospect of adoption and eternal life and glory; but is made to *feel, admire, long for*, and embrace them, quickened to live for that for which it was created, but to which by sin it had become dead, the love, the service, the glory of God. 'For the love of Christ constraineth us.'

Again, the Saviour is food for the *support* of the soul. The soul needs nourishment as well as the body; it must have something to feed its thoughts, to strengthen its powers, to enable it to judge between good and evil, to choose one, and refuse the other. It needs to have its new life sustained by continual supplies of the grace which gave that life at first. Its power to think, feel, and act aright must, as in the case of the body, be supported by supplies from without; neither soul nor body can live and feed upon itself. This support and nourishment is to be had from Christ, and Him only. God hath, as it were, poured into the Saviour the full supply for all the wants of the soul. In Him this supply exists as in a fountain. From Him love, hope, joy, comfort, strength, and all the graces of the Holy Spirit, are to be obtained, and from none else. 'It pleased the Father that in Him should all fulness dwell' (Col. i. 19); 'and in Him dwelleth all the fulness of the Godhead bodily' (Col. ii. 9); 'and,' says St. John (i. 16), 'of His fulness have all we received, and grace for grace.' 'For His flesh is meat *indeed*, and His blood is drink *indeed*.' This food is to be sought for in close, personal intercourse with Christ. The believer must live *with* Christ to live *on* Christ; nay, *He* says not, I have, but 'I am that Bread of life.'

Communion with Christ, Christ Himself, revealed to the soul by the Holy Spirit, is the support of the Christian's life. The more he contemplates, speaks to, hangs on Christ daily, hourly, the stronger, the holier, the happier will he grow. As food, Jesus has in Him a *healing* virtue. Are we troubled by indwelling sin? it is by going to Him we obtain the cure. Where Christ is received into the soul sin cannot reign, Satan's power is broken. Are we suffering under trial of any other kind? the presence of Christ in the soul is the one sure and lasting support and comfort. He is *that* tree of life 'whose leaves are for the healing of the nations' (Rev. xxii. 2). And as pleasant food is a delight to the body, so is Christ the *joy* and *delight* of the renewed soul.

   'Give what Thou wilt, *without Thee* I am poor;
   And *with* Thee rich, take what Thou wilt away.'

It is the believer's delight to think on Jesus, to speak with Jesus, to feel the love of Jesus. He can never have enough of Jesus. 'Blessed are they which do hunger and thirst' after this spiritual food; for He says they shall be filled. And now consider—

II. How Christ is to be received, and the effects of such receiving of Him. He is ascended into heaven; you cannot apply to Him as to earthly food. He cannot be carnally eaten. By the faithful *only He is verily and indeed* taken and received. Thus. I hear of the atonement, believe its power and truth. I go to God, and in faith claim pardon and peace, bought by Christ's body and blood. From that moment I receive the benefit of Christ's redemption, and, 'being justified by faith, have peace with God through our Lord Jesus Christ.' I hear of 'righteousness, temperance, and judgment to come.' I learn of Christ my Saviour's horror of sin, of God the Father's hatred of sin, and of the cross as showing this at the cost of the Saviour's life. I hear of holiness, of His soul being 'exceeding sorrowful, even unto death,' of His life-blood shed for me; and by the power of the Holy Ghost I believe all this to be real; my conscience is stirred up to act. I begin to hate sin, to love Christ, to follow Christ, to live for Christ. New life, an altogether different state of things begins in me. I am learning what it is to agree with St. Paul : 'To me to live is Christ.'

Thus also. It is by faith the Christian goes to Jesus, feeds on Him for the sustenance of his spiritual life, for the healing of the diseases of his soul, and for the delight of a renewed heart. By a believing, praying appropriation to himself of all that Christ has done and is doing, of all that Christ is, and of all that Christ has, the believer really finds the very support, sustenance, comfort, strength, healing, joy and delight he wants. And all this is true and real. Faith and prayer are invisible, but the blessings they bring down are visible in great part even to bodily eyes. Feeding on Christ is a spiritual act; the life, growth, strength, healing, and happiness, derived by the Christian from that food are in a measure visible to all. The process is this: I hear, believe, ask, and receive. Believing, I have life through His name, and that life eternal life; nay, it extends even to the body, for He will raise it up at the last day. 'For whoso eateth My flesh, and drinketh My blood, hath eternal life; and I will raise him up at the last day.'

Consider, in the last place,

III. The reverse of the picture. You who think all these things dreams—you who interpret carnally—you who are too busy to care about them, and you who feed not on Christ, because you feed on ashes, know this, 'Except ye eat the flesh of the Son of man. and drink His blood, ye have no life in you.' No life! *i. e.* eternal death. Oh! that the Holy Ghost would teach you to realise this solemn truth now; that He would cry mightily, 'Awake, thou that sleepest, and arise from the dead.'

Finally, what hath the Holy Communion to

do with this eating and drinking? Probably at the institution of the Lord's Supper, Christ referred to this text. Faith is weak, we need a sign and pledge to assure us of His great love, and this is given to strengthen and refresh our souls. It is an effectual sign, for, received with earnest, expecting faith, it brings unfailing blessing with it. It is to bring to our remembrance His great love in dying for us, and is given for the strengthening and refreshing of our souls, as our bodies are by the bread and wine. 'As often as ye eat this bread, and drink this cup, ye do show\* the Lord's death till He come.'

\* *i. e.* declare: καταγγέλετε.

## IX.

### SAUL THE KING, AND SAUL OF TARSUS.

1 Samuel, x. 11.—'And it came to pass, when all that knew him beforetime saw that, behold, he prophesied among the prophets, then the people said one to another, What is this that has come unto the son of Kish? Is Saul also among the prophets?'

Acts, ix. 26.—'And when Saul was come to Jerusalem, he assayed to join himself to the disciples; but they were all afraid of him, and believed not that he was a disciple.'

CALL up these two great men. Let them pass before you, as they are described in holy Scripture. Behold in imagination the shadowy form of the giant hero-king—higher than any of his subjects from his shoulders and upward. There is none like him among all the people (1 Sam. x. 23, 24). Mark his lion-like bearing and athletic frame, swifter than the eagle, stronger than the lion, says one who knew him well (2 Sam. i. 23). In all his habits the warrior stands confessed; when the nation was disarmed by the Philistines, Saul and Jonathan alone retained their arms. Indeed, we never see him unarmed. In the midst of his palace, as he sits listening to the inspired strains of his harper, his javelin is in his hand. On the festival of the new moon, at his royal table, his javelin lies ready for instant use. In his military excursions, he lies sleeping like a soldier on the ground, among his men, and his spear is stuck in the ground at his head. In battle he takes part not only as general, but as combatant; from the blood of the slain his sword returns not empty (2 Sam. i. 22).

Now bid his namesake and tribesman appear. Lo, Saul of Tarsus stands before you. His poor frame seamed and scarred with the marks of torture and ignominious chastisement. His back indented with the lash, his wrist worn with the chain (Gal. vi. 17). His bodily presence weak, his speech contemptible (2 Cor. x. 10), made as the off-scouring of all things—a spectacle unto the world, and to angels, and to men. The *one*, all that man admires; the *other*, all that man despises. But the Lord seeth not as man seeth. Nevertheless, there were many points of resemblance between these two men. How alike were they in the outset of their career, how alike in natural character. But how great the difference between them in after-life. How far were they asunder in their death?

I have chosen for my text the two verses which I read to you, because they strikingly suggest the comparison to our minds. May the Holy Spirit help us to learn from it some useful lessons.

Saul the king and Saul of Tarsus were men of the same nation, the same tribe; and since they bore the same name, it is probable, as we gather from Jewish customs, that they belonged to the same family (St. Luke, i. 61). We see from their history that they were by nature both of them eager, proud, impetuous, determined. They were alike prompt and quick in action. Saul is chosen king of Israel. So soon as his countrymen are endangered by foreign invasion, a day or two suffices for him to gather together Israel from one end of the land to the other. A forced march brings him to the scene of danger. In the darkness of the night he bursts upon the astonished foe, and by noontide they are so discomfited and scattered that two of them are not left together (1 Sam. xi.). Saul of Tarsus is called to be the Apostle of Him whom a few days before he had persecuted. At once he, like his namesake, rushes to the assault; he, too, breaks into the enemy's camp, and straightway he preached Christ in the synagogues, that He is the Son of God (Acts, ix. 20). Further, there was strong resemblance between these two men in their fervid and earnest patriotism, even if they were sometimes mistaken (one of them *at least*), in their way of manifesting it. Compare King Saul, always in the front rank of battle with his country's enemies, even disregarding justice and humanity, slaying the Gibeonites, to whom Joshua had granted protection, and who were the servants of the Tabernacle, ' in his zeal to the children of Israel and Judah' (2 Sam. xxi. 2). Compare him with Saul of Tarsus, ' I have great heaviness, and continual sorrow in my heart. For I could wish (was wishing) that myself were accursed from Christ for my brethren, my kinsmen according to the flesh; who are Israelites' (Rom. ix. 2–4). Each of them had that in his natural temper which made him a persecutor. Saul hunted David as men hunt a partridge upon the mountains. His namesake stood by as Stephen, Christ's holy martyr, fell asleep beneath the shower of stones ; and was consenting unto his death. King Saul massacred the priests of the Lord. His namesake says of the people of the Lord, ' When they were put to death, I gave my voice against them.' Each of them lived a most eventful life, after being by divine appointment called to the public service of God. And when first so called, such had been the previous life and character of each, that men were astonished at the call, and refused at first to believe in its reality, or in their obedience to it, as we learn from the passages I read as my text. Finally, each of them died by a violent death, and perished by the sword. How *like*, yet how *unlike!* The *one*, a pattern to the Christian; the *other*, a warning to all men. The *one*, a burning and shining light on the way to heaven; the *other*, the red and lurid flame that bids us shun the road which leads to the mouth of the pit. What was the reason of this vast, this all-important difference between them? I believe it lay in this: King Saul, even when he did right, consulted his own will, his own glory, his own pleasure, alone. The other laid down his will, his glory, himself, at the foot of the Cross. The one cries, 'Honour *me* now, before the elders of my people, and before Israel' (1 Sam. xv. 30). The other declares it his earnest expectation and his hope that *Christ* should be magnified in his body, whether by life or by death (Phil. i. 20). King Saul seeks to do that which seems to him best without reference to the commands of God. For instance, when, charged by Samuel with the sin of disobedience in that he had taken on himself to offer sacrifice (to do which was the office of the priest alone, because he was the type of Christ), Saul cannot plead ignorance, he will not confess himself in the wrong. He defends and excuses his disobedience by the plea that he thought it right and necessary to disobey. 'I said, The Philistines will come down now upon me to Gilgal, and I have not made supplication unto the Lord; I forced myself therefore, and offered a burnt-offering. And Samuel said, Thou hast done foolishly; thou hast not kept the commandment of the Lord thy God, which He commanded thee.' (1 Sam. xiii. 12, 13.) So, again, when charged by Samuel with the like sin, in that, while God had commanded him utterly to destroy the sinners, the Amalekites, with all that belonged to them, he had brought with him Agag, the Amalekite monarch, alive along with the best of the spoil; he defends his disobedience instead of seeking pardon for it, or rather, at first, whilst admitting the fact, wholly denies his guilt (1 Sam. xiii. 26).

How different the course pursued by Saul of Tarsus! At the very outset of his new and Christian life, he makes a solemn surrender of himself to the guidance and commandments of God. His first reply to Him that called him from his persecuting course was to pray for teaching, 'Who art Thou, Lord?' his second, to resign his own will unto the power of that Lord, 'Lord, what wilt *Thou* have me to do?' (Acts, ix. 6). And this principle of self-surrender, and mortification of his own will, he carries to such an extent, that when he finds it to be God's will that he shall be kept humble by some infirmity of body, which he calls 'a thorn in the flesh, the messenger of Satan' (permitted by God) 'to buffet me,' he cries, 'Most gladly will I glory in my infirmities' (2 Cor. xii. 9). It is the difference between self-exaltation and self-surrender, between an unsanctified will and a will sanctified by God the Holy Ghost. And what is the result of this difference? The two men are alike placed in great extremity. The *one* says, 'I am sore distressed, for the Philistines make war against me, and God is departed from me, and answereth me no more' (1 Sam. xxviii. 15); the *other*, 'At my first answer no man stood with me, but all men forsook me: I pray God that it may not be laid to their charge. Notwithstanding the Lord stood with me, and strengthened me, and I was delivered out of the mouth of the lion.' (2 Tim. iv. 16, 17.) The *one* says to his armour-bearer, 'Draw thy sword, and thrust me through therewith' (1 Sam. xxxi. 4); the *other*, 'I am now ready to be offered, and the time of my departure is at hand. I have fought a good fight, I have finished my course, I have kept the faith: henceforth there is laid up for me a crown of righteousness, which the Lord, the righteous Judge, shall give me at that day; and not to me only, but unto all them also that love His appearing.' (2 Tim. iv. 6, 7, 8.) The *one* dies by his own sword; and goes to stand before his Judge with the guilt of self-murder on his head; the *other* gives up his life for his Lord, and departs to claim for Jesus' sake the martyr's palm of victory. The *one* wrought no lasting good for Israel, but left them as he found them, defeated and distressed; the *other* has probably been the means of conferring greater blessings on the Church of Christ than any other man that ever lived.

Learn, brethren, that if you would fulfil aright the duties of your station, you must in all seek the glory of God, and not your own.

We confess that this is just, since ' He died for us all, that they which live should not henceforth live unto themselves, but unto Him which died for them and rose again' (2 Cor. v. 15). We confess it, but how little do we act according to this rule!

Brethren, let us pray for grace to *watch* over the motives of all we do, to strive hard to set aside the desire of honour and credit for ourselves, and to aim at glorifying Him who bought us with His blood. Learn, also, that not only *sinful* self, but *wilful* self, is to be resigned to God. Not only *my* will to do evil, but my will to do what *I* think best for His service must be subdued to the will of God. In all I must follow my Saviour's example. ' Not my will, but

Thine be done.' If I would do great things for His name's sake, the great things must be such as *He* sets before me; and if it is His will to set me to the meanest work for Him, I must be contented. I must try to do the duty He lays before me as He bids me do it, not as I think best to do it. Even in prayer, my will is to bow in submission before His. Simple, implicit, unswerving obedience is required at our hands. 'To obey is better than sacrifice.'

> 'The best will is our Father's will,
> And we may rest there calm and still;
> Oh, make it hour by hour thine own,
> And wish for nought but that alone,
>       Which pleases God.' *

'Lord, what wilt Thou have me to do?' is the true spirit of Christian service. He who sets out in this spirit, in reliance only on the Holy Ghost, shall not be destitute of guidance and direction. How soon was that prayer answered in the case of Saul of Tarsus! 'It shall be told thee what thou must do.'

\* Paul Gerhardt.

## X.

### CHRISTIAN CONFIDENCE AND CHRISTIAN DUTY.

Acts, xxvii., latter part of 23rd verse.—'Whose I am, and whom I serve.'

A GREAT corn ship, bound from Egypt to Italy, was lying-to in a Levant gale. Unwieldy,—as were the merchant-vessels of the ancients,—and damaged by the violence of the storm. Her condition was such that, as St. Luke, who was on board, says, all hope that they should be saved was taken away. At that time they had not the mariner's compass, but directed their course by observations of the sun and stars. As, however, often happens in these gales, the sky was for many days overclouded, and neither sun nor stars could be seen, so that no observations could be made which might give them information as to their position. All that the officers and crew could tell was that they were in danger of being driven upon the fatal quicksands of the north coast of Africa. They had done their utmost to relieve the labouring and straining of the ship; they had cast overboard whatever could be spared, including some at least of the ship's tackling. To prevent her frame from giving way they had passed a cable several times round her, as has been done in extreme cases even in modern days. They had on board a military officer of rank, with a guard of soldiers, and a number of prisoners in charge; a helpless multitude, who, with one exception presently to be noticed, could do little but add to the general confusion and distress. We can picture to ourselves their misery as day after day of hardship and trial passed, and the storm gave no signs of abating. Weak with fasting, for they probably had neither courage nor opportunity to prepare food, worn with toil, harassed by the wet and cold, they were in despair. At that hour of hopeless terror there stood forth in the midst of them one of the prisoners, who, undaunted by the violence of the storm, thus, before a heathen ship's company, testified to his unshaken trust in the one true God (vers. 21–25): 'Sirs, ye should have hearkened unto me, and not have loosed from Crete, and to have gained this harm and loss. And now I exhort you to be of good cheer: for there shall be no loss of any man's life among you, but of the ship. For there stood by me this night the angel of God, Whose I am, and Whom I serve, saying, Fear not, Paul; thou must be brought before Cæsar: and, lo, God hath given thee all them that sail with thee.' To this declaration the words of our text serve, as it were, as the key-note. They explain the confidence of this noble prisoner. It was the consciousness that he was the Lord's, and engaged in the Lord's service, that enabled him to say, amidst the raging of the winds and waves, ' Sirs, be of good cheer; for I believe God, that it shall be even as it was told me.'

'Whose I am, and whom I serve.' The words lead us from the Christian up to his God. It was upon the character and attributes of this God that the Apostle rested so calmly in the hour of trial. He had said, 'Fear not, for I have redeemed thee, I have called thee by thy name; thou art mine. When thou passest through the waters, I will be with thee, and through the rivers, they shall not overflow thee.' (Isa. xliii. 1, 2.) And St. Paul knew Him to be the Lord God, holy and true. He described Him as ' God that cannot lie.' (Titus, i. 2.) He knew now that from age to age God's promises had never failed, and that not one of all those who had put their trust in Him had ever been confounded. He would very possibly remember the reply of the glorious three to Nebuchadnezzar, as they stood by the mouth of the burning fiery furnace:

'*Our God whom we serve*' is able to deliver us from the burning fiery furnace, and He will deliver us out of thine hand, O king.' (Dan. iii. 17.) And he knew how, to justify their confidence, the Son of God Himself came down and walked in the furnace by their side. Hence when the angel of God came to him and said, 'Fear not, Paul; lo, God hath given thee all them that sail with thee,'—though the sea wrought and was tempestuous, yet the Apostle was assured of their safety. He had good ground for the assertion, 'I believe God, that it shall be even as it was told me.' (ver. 25.)

Brethren, let us try by grace more fully to realise this attribute of our God—*His faithfulness*. It is the very foundation of the Christian life. If we could but take God at His word, how many hindrances to our growth in grace would be removed; how many doubts and cares and anxieties should we be spared! It were a good thing for us to study more thoughtfully the character of God as displayed to us in the histories of Holy Scripture. We should store up the many instances in which He justified the confidence of His servants of old. Then, in days when all is dark around us, when there are no visible signs of deliverance, when 'neither sun nor stars appear,' we should be enabled to rest for time and eternity upon His unchanging power, love, and truth, and to join our voices with that of the afflicted patriarch Job, 'Though He slay me, yet will I trust in Him.'

'Whose I am!' From this knowledge that he is God's arises another argument on which St. Paul's confidence is based. A poor possession for his Maker, if regarded in itself. Worthless in itself before Him, Who could in a moment create and people a new world by His word alone. 'I belong to Him!' the Christian may say; yet must he not confess, 'I am not worthy to be owned by Him; I am but dust and ashes in His sight?' How, then, can this ownership on God's part be any reason why we should trust Him to care for us?

My brethren, the answer lies *in the price* His mercy paid to save us from His justice. It comes from the cross. It is to be heard in the agonising cry, 'My God, My God, why hast Thou forsaken Me?' It was to save us; it was that *we* might *not* be forsaken in our time of need. For *our* sins *He* suffered, for our unworthiness He gave His worthiness. God had one thing that He prized above all else in heaven or earth. God's love for His Son passes all understanding, and that Son He gave up for us men and for our salvation. That was the price He paid to win the very vilest among us, that every one who would simply trust in Him might be able to say, with firm, humble confidence, 'Whose I am.' I say humble confidence, for the great and glorious truth itself is deeply humbling to proud human nature. All boasting is excluded. I am nothing worth save for the price *He* paid for me.

Yet, brethren, what a grand basis for trust we have here! Did the Father give for us His most precious treasure? Did the Son give Himself for us, and shall we fear to rely on Him for time or for eternity? He bought me with His blood; will He deny me any good thing? He gave Himself for me; will He ever cast me away? He lived to win me; will He not preserve me all my days? He died that I might be His; shall I not be His in death? He is alive for evermore; will He not for evermore preserve in life those who cost Him so much?

'Whose I am.' Here, also, is the basis of the Christian's confidence in prayer. 'I am Thine; save me' (Ps. cxix. 94), is the language of the Psalmist, and should be the plea of each believing soul, especially in times of distress. Spare Thy servant whom Thou hast redeemed with Thy most precious blood.

'Whose I am!' This, too, is our confidence in death: 'Whether we live or die, we are the

Lord's.' (Rom. xiv. 9.) Hence it is that the expiring Christian is enabled to say with David, 'Into Thy hands I commit my spirit, for Thou hast redeemed me, O Lord God of truth.' (Ps. xxxi. 5.) And so saying, like holy Stephen the martyr, to fall asleep and go to rest in Jesus. But it may be asked, Does God respond to this confidence shown on the part of His servants? Does He warrant and encourage it? I reply by another question. What is the meaning of such language as this, 'Of them which Thou gavest Me have I lost none?' (St. John, xviii. 9.) 'Holy Father, keep through Thine own name those whom Thou hast given Me.' (St. John, xvii. 11.) 'My sheep shall never perish, neither shall any man pluck them out of My hand.' (St. John, x. 27, 28.) And, to crown all, that glorious assurance as to the day of judgment: 'They shall be Mine, saith the Lord of hosts, in that day when I make up My jewels. And I will spare them as a man spareth his own son that serveth him.' (Mal. iii. 17.) What a response to the Christian's declaration, 'Whose I am!'

The second clause of the text follows naturally: 'Whom I serve' is the true sequence of 'Whose I am.' None can truly serve Him but such as are His, saved by His self-sacrifice, created anew by His Holy Spirit. As it is written, 'This people have I formed for Myself; they shall show forth My praise.' (Isa. xliii. 21.) Look, then, to *this* for the evidence of your being Christ's. Are you striving, in reliance on the power of the Holy Ghost, to do His will? Can you say of yourselves, each as in His sight, 'Whom I serve?' 'Ye shall know them' (says Christ) 'by their fruits. Do men gather grapes of thorns, or figs of thistles? Even so every good tree bringeth forth good fruit.' (St. Matt. vii. 16, 17.)

But further, we have in the text our *strongest motive* to Christian duty. 'His I am, *therefore* Him I *must* serve.' And this service is not accomplished by the power of flesh and blood; for at the outset it demands the quelling of our own nature, with all its evil tempers and desires. 'Whose I am.' Is it so? *Then*, 'they that are Christ's have *crucified* the flesh with the affections and lusts.' (Gal. v. 24.) 'Whom I serve.' Is it so? *Then*, 'if any man serve Me, let him *follow* Me' (St. John, xii. 26); and, 'If any man will come after Me, let him *deny* himself, and take up his cross daily, and follow Me.' (St. Luke, ix. 23.)

All this, brethren, requires such a continual warfare, such a life-long struggle, as can only be accomplished in the power of the Holy Ghost. Thank God, He has promised to give the Holy

Ghost to them that ask Him! But vast as is the sacrifice, great the task of fulfilling those words, 'Whom I serve,' ample motives are supplied us. We find them in the privileges of those other words, 'Whose I am,' and in the price paid that they might be true. 'Ye were not redeemed with corruptible things, as silver and gold, but with the precious blood of Christ.' (1 St. Pet. i. 18, 19.) 'Ye are not your own; for ye are bought with a price; therefore glorify God in your body, and in your spirit, which are God's.' (1 Cor. vi. 19. 20.)

Lastly, St. Paul instructs us here not to be ashamed to confess the faith of Christ crucified. O rich man, tempted by fear of ridicule to hide your faith in Christ, to be ashamed of religion in society, drawn to comply with a careless world in various matters which you know are *wrong*, as tried by the word of God, but you cannot bear to differ from the rest.—I charge you, as you value eternity, pray for grace, at home and abroad, in business, in company, living and dying, to let this be seen as the principle of your soul's life. 'Whose I am, and whom I serve.' Call to mind the first minister of state of the great empire of Babylon,—how on his whole character and life those words, 'Whose I am, and whom I serve,' were so plainly inscribed that the heathen king Darius, while feeling bound by an evil law to sacrifice him, thus addressed him as he went to the lions' den, '*Thy God, whom thou servest* continually, He will deliver thee.' (Dan. vi. 16.) And you, my brother, obliged to toil for a living among many who charge you with a pretence of religion for gain's sake, with folly, hypocrisy, enthusiasm, let this be your memorial, this your rule by grace, '*Whose I am, and whom I serve.*' And all of you remember that prisoner on the great ship's deck, as he stood among a band of heathen, and amid the wash of the waves, and the howling of the storm, lifted up his voice and owned his Lord, 'Whose I am, and whom I serve.'

O Christian people, why was the cross in infancy signed upon your foreheads? Was it not in token of earnest prayer and solemn covenant that each of you should bear stamped upon his life and conversation. 'Whose I am, and whom I serve?'

## XI.

### NEGLECTED OPPORTUNITIES.

St. Matthew, xxvi., part of verse 45.—'Sleep on now and take your rest.'

THE subject of good works is one that needs much caution in its treatment by the ministers of Christ. We have to be on our guard lest we remove them from their proper place in the economy of salvation, lest we speak of them as if in any way they could form a part of the price of our redemption. Yet we must beware of making light of those things which are in the sight of God of great price. For good works are not only *to us* the evidence that we are grafted into the true vine, living branches thereof, real members of Christ; but they are also *to God* the fruits of His Spirit, clusters from His vineyard. He comes to that vineyard seeking such fruits from every tree that is planted therein. Of each He says, 'If it bear fruit, well.' To each of His servants, who is abundant in good works, He will by-and-by proclaim from the seat of judgment,

'Well done! good and faithful.' Christ did, indeed, buy us with His righteousness and His own most precious blood. This was the *only* price of our redemption: He made on the Cross a full, perfect, and sufficient sacrifice, oblation, and satisfaction for the sins of the whole world. No man can add to that salvation, none can take from it. 'It is finished.' Whosoever will accept that salvation by faith finds eternal life. 'He that believeth on Him is not condemned,' but 'is passed from death unto life.' Yet, brethren, let us remember that Christ bought us for *Himself*, to follow *His* example, and be made like unto *Him*. He glorified His Father, not only in suffering according to His will, but also by doing His work. His life was a life of good works: 'He went about doing good.'

To follow Him in *this* is our privilege as well as our duty.

To strengthen us for *this* He sends us the Holy Ghost from heaven. To judge of *this* work of ours He will sit on the throne at the great day, and in proportion to our prayerful diligence in *this* work will be the brightness of our crown. 'Behold,' He says, 'I come quickly, and my reward is with me, to give every man according as his work shall be.' (Rev. xxii. 12.) Now as 'to everything there is a season, and a time to every purpose under heaven' (Eccles. iii. 1), so in this matter of good works there are times and opportunities for their performance, given and appointed by God. And these times come to an end, these opportunities are limited. It was so even with our Lord Himself in His life on earth. 'I must,' said He, 'work the work of Him that sent Me while it is day; the night cometh when no man can work.' (St. John, ix. 4.)

It is so in the life of the Christian. There is a time to labour, and a time to rest—a time in which we may, by the grace of the Holy Spirit, labour for the glory of Him that bought us with His blood.—a time during which we may, for His sake, strive for the spiritual and temporal welfare of fellow-sinners and of fellow-sufferers; a time in which we may thus work the works of Him that called us; yet a limited time,—'while it is day.'

The faithful labourer for God and for his brethren, wearied with the burden of the day, is called to his repose in Paradise; he takes his rest, he sleeps in Jesus, until he is brought again at that day in glory with his Lord. And blessed are all such as having fought the good fight, finished their course, and kept the faith, do rest from their labours; their works do follow them. But, brethren, it is no summons to this sacred rest that we find in our text. There is such a thing as sleeping through the whole, or a part of our set time for work; sleeping while it is day when night is coming on.

Oh, depth of mercy for such, if they awake in time and find pardon at the foot of the cross, and are snatched as brands from the burning, though their work for the Crucified be all undone! Others who are Christians too often permit the sleep of inactivity to overcome them while they should be working. Presently they are aroused with grief and shame to see their life's sun high in the meridian, or perhaps dipping in the west, while they have slumbered; to find times and occasions for service, past and unused, and never to be recovered. It may be said, sadly enough to them, 'Sleep on now, and take your rest;' your opportunity is dead and gone.

It was thus with the disciples. They were led by the Lord to be with Him in the night of the betrayal, in the garden of Gethsemane.

To three of them He addressed that most wonderful appeal for sympathy with Himself in His mental anguish on behalf of sinners, for whom He was going to die, 'My soul is exceeding sorrowful even unto death; tarry ye here and watch with me.' Did they hear those words? Could it be that at that hour of His deepest misery they slept, and, though awakened by their suffering Master, they slept again? What an honour it was to be chosen by the Son of Man to be at His side in this agony! What an exalted privilege it would have been to comfort Him by their sympathy, to sustain His human nature by joining their prayers with His, and to use as surely they might well have used the language of prophetic supplication for Him, 'The Lord hear Thee in the day of trouble, the name of the God of Jacob defend Thee. Send Thee help from the sanctuary, and strengthen Thee out of Zion. Remember all Thy offerings, and accept Thy burnt *sacrifice*. Grant Thee according to thine own heart, and fulfil all thy counsel' (Ps. xx. 1–4.) What joy to them in after-life if they could have remembered that they had been enabled to render thus some of the last offices of love to their anguish-stricken Saviour. This was not to be. They suffered sleep to overcome them. When thoroughly aroused by His voice they awoke to find the occasion for loving service over, past and gone. For other ministrations there might still be gracious opportunities, but for *that* special offering of love to Him in His agony, the opportunity was no more. As concerning that, let them sleep on now and take their rest. But in after days would they not often think with bitter sorrow that when their Lord asked of them that hour's watch with Him in prayer, in that He feared, they had yielded to nature's weakness, and had slumbered? 'Sleep on *now* and take your rest.' Sad, solemn words that may well be taken as a requiem of departed opportunities.

Our time, brethren, for service is limited, and not to be extended; our occasions for *special services* cannot be recalled. An hour in which we might have glorified God, or done good to man, strikes only once. If we lose it, we may by the Holy Spirit's help employ the next in work for Christ; but *that* hour is lost for ever. An opportunity for holy duty neglected may be followed by another of the *same kind*, yet it will *not* be the *same* that is gone. As to *that*, ' Sleep on now and take your rest.' Our Saviour immediately adds, ' Rise, let us be going; behold, he is at hand that doth betray me.' As if He had said, ' You have lost one opportunity of service; in mercy I give you another: you lost your permission to watch with Me in My agony; I give you permission to stand by Me in My betrayal; to cleave to Me in the Palace of the Chief Priest, in the Judgment Hall, and at the cross of Calvary.' But this gracious offer could not erase from their memory that sad utterance of a wounded heart, ' What could ye not watch with Me one hour?' 'Sleep on *now*, and take your rest.'

My brethren, you who desire to serve God let me impress upon you the necessity of asking grace, to do each hour's duty *in* its hour, to use each opportunity of service *as it occurs*. How *many* of these are granted to most of us in the course of our lives! How often, for instance, has each Christian an opportunity of speaking to other men on his Lord's behalf, of commending to them the Saviour whom he has himself found, of pointing them to the blood by which their sins were expiated, and saying to them in some way, 'Behold the Lamb of God.' Who among us is there that has not had it in his power to deny himself, for his Lord's sake and his brethren's, rest, or ease, or something on which he would have liked to spend money or effort; but Christ has condescended to say, 'The Lord hath need of it?' He never personally appealed to us for help and sympathy in hours of trial; yet has He not many a time given us opportunity to bestow that help and sympathy on Him in the person of His people, and, guiding us to the side of some suffering Christian, has He not said, 'Tarry ye here, and watch with Me?' O brethren, have we not too often let slip these opportunities of service? And now they are gone, past recovery,— 'Sleep on now, and take your rest!' They are never to return. Many a son or daughter here can remember the day when it was in his or her power to minister comfort and help to a parent in want of both, to watch and pray by the side of a sick or dying father or mother. And, alas!

too many must confess, 'I did not do all I might have done. I consulted my ease rather than my duty, and now God has taken my parents away: now He seems to say, "Sleep on now, and take your rest," they whom you might have comforted will need your help no more.'

My brethren, time will not permit me even to *attempt* to set before you all the opportunities that God has given us for holy duty. If conscience reminds us how often we have had them and neglected them till they were withdrawn,—if memory reproaches us, and says to us, 'Sleep on now, and take your rest,' yet may grace sanctify our sorrow, and point us, first, to the cross of Christ for the pardon of past 'sins, negligences, and ignorances' of this kind, and then to the words of our Lord, 'Rise, let us be going.' Though it be sad, indeed, to look back upon the past, and to see the good works that we might have done, but have left undone; yet let those words impress upon us the duty in time to come, if time be given us, of watching and prayer, against negligence in the path of obedience. Let us strive, in a strength not our own, to redeem the time that remains. 'Watch and pray.' And you who know and feel that these opportunities of service have been given also to you, but have been neglected by you, because you neither love the Lord Jesus nor care to serve Him, O, how will you bear in the great day to see displayed before you all the good you might have done, but left undone, all the means of grace offered you which you despised, each call of mercy from which you turned away, the Saviour Himself, who offered Himself to you, but Whom you rejected? You slumbered in soul, and took your rest, such as it was, in worldliness and in sin. How will you bear to hear the sentence, 'Sleep on now, and take your rest,' if you *can* rest, amid eternal woe. You will be awake then, but awake too late! To-day, while it is called to-day, harden not your hearts.

# XII.

## THE REQUIREMENTS OF GOD.

Micah, vi. 8.—'He hath showed thee, O man, what is good; and what doth the Lord require of thee, but to do justly, and to love mercy, and to walk humbly with thy God?'

THE text declares that God 'hath showed us' these things; where? In His holy word. Let us consult that word on each of these three points, and learn from some examples, at least, the general bearing of each, and the spirit in which each is to be obeyed.

I. Do justly. To act, speak, and to strive to think fairly, honestly, towards all men. Not to suffer feelings, interest, passions, or prejudices to influence us. Men have strange notions as to justice. Many would think it very hard to be told that, to depart from strict justice in favour of a friend or relation, is a grievous sin; or, that many common practices of trade are enough to sink their souls to perdition; or, that many things that can be done without breaking the law of man are violations of the law of God. See what God says as to favouring any one above another in a matter between them. Deut. xvi. 19, 20: 'Thou shalt not wrest judgment, thou shalt not respect persons, neither take a gift: for a gift doth blind the eyes of the wise, and pervert the words of the righteous. That which is altogether just shalt thou follow, that thou mayest live, and inherit the land which the Lord thy God giveth thee.' 'Not respect persons!' any persons, friends, relations, foes, or strangers? Thou shalt be just to the poor, that cannot reward thee. Ps. lxxxii. 3, 4: 'Defend the poor and fatherless: do justice to the afflicted and needy. Deliver the poor and needy; rid them out of the hand of the wicked.'

Yet thou mayest not strain a point in favour of the poor if he be in the wrong, nor let pity blind thine eyes to justice. Exod. xxiii. 3: 'Neither shalt thou countenance a poor man in his cause.' This principle is universal in application. *E.g.* in a contested election, no respect of persons should be allowed, no favouring of those who have served you. You are bound to vote for such as are best qualified, in your opinion, to fill the post. Selling a vote for present pay or future expectations is a sin against this law of God; it is a respect of persons; it is also directly forbidden. Exod. xxiii. 8: 'And thou shalt take no gift; for the gift blindeth the wise, and perverteth the words of the righteous.' The stranger and foreigner is to receive the same justice from us as our nearest friend, nay, as we would desire for ourselves. Lev. xix. 33, 34: 'And if a stranger sojourn with you in your land, ye shall not vex him. But the stranger that dwelleth with you shall be unto you as one born amongst you, and thou shalt love him as thyself; for ye were strangers in the land of Egypt: I am the Lord your God.' And thus in all our dealings with others we are to have respect to the right only, and no respect of persons is allowed; we are not even suffered to depart from the strict right as members of a society or a party. Exod. xxiii. 2: 'Thou shalt not follow a multitude to do evil; neither shalt thou speak in a cause to decline after many, to wrest judgment.'

Again, in business dealings I fear that many things are common which are most hateful to Almighty God because they are not just:—adulterations, the light weight, inferior goods with an outside show of value. What saith the Lord? Lev. xix. 35, 36: 'Ye shall do no unrighteousness in judgment, in meteyard, in weight, or in measure. Just balances, just weights, a just ephah, and a just hin, shall ye have: I am the Lord your God, which brought you out of the land of Egypt.' Nor think that such sins are confined to the seller. Who thinks any harm of a bargain? Who does not boast of his cleverness, and of his gains therein? Yet is it unjust before God. Prov. xx. 14: 'It is naught, it is naught, saith the buyer: but when he is gone his way, then he boasteth.' How many practices that man's law cannot reach are condemned as unjust by such texts as Lev. xix. 11: 'Ye shall not steal, neither deal falsely, neither lie one to another;' and also in Exod. xxiii. 1: 'Thou shalt not raise a false report: put not thine hand with the wicked, to be an unrighteous witness.' How strict are God's demands for justice between all men!—Masters to servants, 'that which is just and equal.' Servants to masters, 'not with eye-service, as men-pleasers.' Children to parents, 'obey in the Lord.' Parents to children, 'provoke not your children to wrath.'

Dear brethren, let us ask God to send His Holy Spirit to enable us to take pains to find out that which is just and equal, and to strengthen us fearlessly to follow it, acting in the spirit of the examples I have just quoted. How often have we deviated from this path of strict justice! Let the thought lead us to Christ. 1 St. Pet. iii. 18: 'For Christ also hath once suffered for sins, the just for the unjust, that He might bring us to God.' I will only remark further on this part of my subject, that we are bidden to *do* justly, but not commanded always to *exact* justice or our strict rights from others. Rather, to enter into the spirit of the next command—

II. ' Love mercy.' Notice the change of expression : *Do* justice, *love* mercy. God Himself, while He loves justice (the cross shows how much), yet is not represented as taking pleasure in executing the sentences which His justice demands. Such work is called His ' strange work.' (Isa. xxviii. 21.) ' For the Lord shall rise up as in Mount Perazim; He shall be wroth, as in the valley of Gibeon, that He may do His work, His strange work ; and bring to pass His act, His strange act.' And, says the prophet Jeremiah in Lam. iii. 33, ' For He doth not afflict willingly nor grieve the children of men.' Whereas of His mercy we are told that ' God is love ;' and (Micah, vii. 18), ' Who is a God like unto Thee, that pardoneth iniquity and passeth by the transgression of the remnant of His heritage ? He retaineth not His anger for ever, because He delighteth in mercy.'

So to the Christian, the doing of strict justice is sometimes most painful, but the work of mercy is ever a labour of love. He feels that in this work he is especially following his Saviour. He learns too, more and more, how much he is indebted to mercy,—mercy incarnate, as it were, in our Lord Jesus; and hence He loves mercy with thankful love, and the work of mercy is to him the work of gratitude. Let us turn to the Bible for a few of the many beautiful precepts on the subject which it affords. For instance, if an opportunity of doing a work of mercy occurs, the servant of God will not let it pass by because he can do so without its being known. He loves mercy, and will gladly show it. Deut. xxii. 1–4 : 'Thou shalt not see thy brother's ox or his sheep go astray, and hide thyself from them : thou shalt in any case bring them to thy brother. And if thy brother be not nigh unto thee, or if thou know him not, then thou shalt bring it unto thine own house, and it shall be with thee until thy brother seek after it, and thou shalt restore it to him again. In like manner shalt thou do with his ass; and so shalt thou do with his raiment, and with all lost things of thy brother's which he hath lost, and thou hast found, shalt thou do likewise. Thou shalt not see thy brother's ass or his ox fall down by the way, and hide thyself from them : thou shalt surely help him to lift them up again.' A godly man will not let slip an opportunity of showing mercy to his enemy. Exod. xxiii. 4, 5 : 'If thou meet thine enemy's ox or his ass going astray, thou shalt surely bring it back to him again. If thou see the ass of him that hateth thee lying under his burden, and wouldest forbear to help him, thou shalt surely help with him.' Indeed, a Christian is to do all the good in his power to his enemies. St. Matt. v. 44: 'But I say unto you, Love your enemies, bless them that curse you, do good to them that hate you, and pray for them which despitefully use you and persecute you.' And in Rom. xii. 20, 21: 'Therefore if thine enemy hunger, feed him; if he thirst, give him drink: for in so doing thou shalt heap coals of fire on his head. Be not overcome of evil, but overcome evil with God.'

The poor are the especial objects of God's mercy. Deut. xv. 11: 'For the poor shall never cease out of the land: therefore I command thee, saying, Thou shalt open thine hand wide unto thy brother, to thy poor, and to thy needy, in thy land.' Mark the words *thy poor*.' Yet in this also must we *do justly*, not helping the idle and unworthy, while the honest and deserving are in need, nor giving to the poor what we owe to our creditors. It is the part of the merciful to act with delicacy and tenderness towards the poor and unfortunate. A beautiful command is given us in Deut. xxiv. 10–13: 'When thou dost lend thy brother any thing, thou shalt not go into his house to fetch his pledge. Thou shalt stand abroad, and the man to whom thou dost lend shall bring out the pledge abroad unto thee. And if the man be poor, thou shalt not sleep with his pledge: in any case thou shalt deliver him the pledge again when the sun goeth down, that he may sleep in his own raiment, and bless thee; and it shall be righteousness unto thee before the Lord thy God.'

Moreover the merciful will not be too sharp in gathering for himself all he can, nor in insisting on every right which man's law gives him, if that right bear hardly on his neighbour. Deut. xxiv. 19–21: 'When thou cuttest down thine harvest in thy field, and hast forgot a sheaf in the field, thou shalt not go again to fetch it: it shall be for the stranger, for the fatherless, and for the widow; that the Lord thy God may bless thee in all the work of thine hands. When thou beatest thine olive tree, thou shalt not go over the boughs again: it shall be for the stranger, for the fatherless, and for the widow.' This reference speaks to us on the first point. And as to the second point *man* may say, Surely I have a right to all the law allows me: but God says (St. James, ii. 13), 'For he shall have judgment without mercy that hath showed no mercy; and mercy rejoiceth against judgment.'

Remember, too, that mercy is to be shown

in sympathy. Rom. xii. 15: 'Rejoice with them that do rejoice, and weep with them that weep.' And, to descend to the lowest of God's creatures, the merciful man is merciful to his beast. Would you learn to love mercy, look at it as exemplified in the person and character of Christ our Saviour. 'Neither do I condemn thee; go and sin no more' (St. John, viii. 11), to a sinner for whom He was going to die; and for His murderers, 'Father, forgive them, for they know not what they do.' (St. Luke, xxiii. 34.) You will *love mercy* if you have obtained Christ's *infinite mercy*.

III. 'Walk humbly with thy God.' The humblest thing a man can do is to accept Christ only, Christ simply, Christ as his all. Have you, dear brethren, thus accepted Christ the Saviour? The next is to depend simply and entirely on God the Holy Ghost for strength to do justly, grace to love mercy, and to walk humbly. Are you thus seeking? A humble walk with God presupposes that a man has taken the Lord for *his* God, and *is* seeking to walk with Him. To walk humbly is to have a constant sense of our sinfulness,—God's holiness, our weakness,—God's all might, our folly and ignorance,—God's wisdom, truth, and love. It is to acknowledge God in prosperity. Deut. viii. 12, &c.: 'Lest when thou hast eaten and art full, and hast built goodly houses, and dwelt therein; and when thy herds and thy flocks multiply, and thy silver and thy gold is multiplied, and all that thou hast is multiplied; then thine heart be lifted up, and thou forget the Lord thy God, which brought thee forth out of the Land of Egypt, from the house of bondage. Who led thee through that great and terrible wilderness, wherein were fiery serpents and scorpions and drought, where there was no water; who brought thee forth water out of the rock of flint; who fed thee in the wilderness with manna, which thy fathers knew not, that He might humble thee, and that He might prove thee, to do thee good at thy latter end; and thou say in thine heart, My power, and the might of mine hand, hath gotten me this wealth. But thou shalt remember the Lord thy God: for it is He that giveth thee power to get wealth.'

It is to acknowledge God in adversity. 1 St. Pet. v. 6: 'Humble yourselves, therefore, under the mighty hand of God, that He may exalt you in due time.' So by grace walking, you will walk with God and God with you. Isa. lvii. 15: 'For thus saith the high and lofty One that inhabiteth eternity, whose name is Holy; I dwell in the high and holy place, with him also that is of a contrite and humble spirit, to revive the spirit of the humble, and to revive the heart of the contrite ones.'

In conclusion, do not the passages I have read to you convince us of the beauty of the word of God, and justify the assertion, 'God hath showed thee, O man, what is good?' Remember, God requires us thus to walk and to serve Him. Past failure to obey must be laid on Christ, so must future failures; yet for the time to come seek grace of the Holy Ghost, that this text may be a law unto you: 'He hath showed thee, O man, what is good; and what doth the Lord require of thee, but to do justly, and to love mercy, and to walk humbly with thy God.'

## XIII.

### THE CANAANITE MOTHER.

St. Matthew, xv., part of verse 28.—'O woman, great is thy faith, be it unto thee, even as thou wilt.'

'WHY should I pray?' says the sceptic. 'God knows all my wants, better than I can tell Him. I will leave them to Him. It is presumption to suppose that He needs information upon the subject, or that He must be entreated, in order that He may be led to do that which is right and good for me.' My brethren, it is quite a sufficient answer to this argument to reply: God has *commanded* us to pray, and has *appointed* prayer to be the means of obtaining our desires from Him. It might be added that prayer is the irrepressible expression of nature's yearning desire for that which we hold to be good, and after Him Who can, we believe, bestow that good upon us; the agonised cry of a fallen, suffering, dying world to its Creator. But one most important aspect of prayer is frequently lost sight of, and that is, its reflex action upon him that prays, altogether irrespective of the obtaining of that object for which he prays. When David had prayed for hardened offenders, and perceived that his prayer had been of no avail for *them*, yet he owns that it had brought a blessing on himself, and declares, 'My prayer returned into mine own bosom.' (Ps. xxxv. 13.) Prayer brings the spirit of man into close and intimate contact with the Father of spirits. Prayer leads him to hold communion with the God of infinite purity and holiness, of almighty power, and wisdom unsearchable, the God of love. Surely such intercourse must exert a blessed influence upon the mind of him that prays. It cannot fail to elevate and to refine, to sanctify and purify, his soul. Again, prayer brings into exercise many of the highest gifts of the Divine Spirit to man. It awakens to activity, faith and trust, humility, patience, hope and love, reverence and submission.

It intensifies them by exercise, and proves to us their value. Can we, then, wonder at the earnestness with which the duty of prayer is impressed upon us in Holy Scripture, or, shall we be surprised if God is sometimes pleased to prolong so profitable an engagement of our highest faculties, by withholding for a while the granting of our petitions? The history of which the text forms a part is calculated in a remarkable degree to illustrate these truths. The person who, on this occasion, sought our Lord's help was a Canaanite or Syrophenician woman. She had probably spent her life in constant communication with her Jewish neighbours, as we see from her language. She was aware that they expected a Deliverer, who should be in some sense divine, and yet be a descendant of the royal house of David. She must have also heard a report that these expectations were fulfilled in Jesus of Nazareth. By personal observation, or by the accounts which had reached her of His words and deeds of wisdom, power, and mercy, she was convinced that this report was true. And now in her deep affliction she comes to Him for relief. She proves at once her knowledge of His person and character, and her faith in His power and love, by the mode of her address, 'Have mercy on me, O Lord, thou Son of David, my daughter is grievously vexed with a devil' (St. Matt. xv. 22.) The ultimate result of her application to Him was remarkable, full of mercy and of love even towards *her*. Christ appears at first to take no notice of her. He answers her not a word. The disciples, probably aware of their Master's desire for privacy (St. Mark, vii. 24), and annoyed by her persistent importunity, request Him to deliver them from her presence: 'Send her away, for she crieth after us,' *i.e.*, grant her petition that

that we may be rid of her. He speaks now, but His words, usually so gentle, must have seemed very hard to her; 'I am not sent but to the lost sheep of the house of Israel.' The time was not yet come when He would charge His servants to go into all the world and preach the Gospel to every creature.

We should have expected that this sentence would suffice to send her away in despair and, it may be, murmuring, at the exclusiveness of that Gospel which brought no mercy to *her*. Her Saviour knew her better. He watched her wondrous faith stirred up and strengthened by refusal and delay. He suffered her cross to lie upon her still, since it brought her nearer to Him. Then came she and worshipped Him, saying, 'Lord, help me.' In His infinite love He yet holds back. He adds reproach to refusal, making use of a Jewish proverbial expression concerning the Gentiles: 'It is not meet to take the children's bread and cast it to dogs.' There must have been a mighty work of Divine grace in her poor aching heart to produce her meek reply. She accepts the reproach, and takes it to herself, but still she believes, still she hopes, still she prays. Our Lord had used a word signifying not the wild and savage dogs which haunted and still haunt the streets of Eastern cities, such dogs as devoured the body of Jezebel, and licked the sores of

Lazarus; but the tame dogs of the house, the despised yet familiar servants of the Master. With eager readiness she catches at that word (κυνάρια). Truth, the Jews are God's children, the table is spread for them, the banquet is theirs, yet there may be out of their rich abundance a fragment for me. If I be not a child, if I be but a dog, yet the children's father is *my Master*. 'Truth, Lord, yet the dogs eat of the crumbs which fall from *their master's* table.' For a small moment He hath hid His face from her, that with greater mercy He may show kindness unto her. He has tried and proved the faith which He Himself had given her; He has exercised the patience, perseverance, and deep humility with which his own spirit had inspired her. He has led her into direct personal intercourse with Himself. He has taught her a blessed lesson, which she will never forget, He has taught her how to pray. *Now* He will crown all His goodness to her by bestowing on her His approval, and granting her request. 'O woman, great is thy faith; be it unto thee even as thou wilt; and her daughter was made whole from that very hour.' How great the blessing of pain and sorrow, how glorious the triumphs of adversity, when these are sanctified to be the means of bringing back fallen and rebellious man to his God and Saviour, when they drive him to seek refuge in the Lord. Consider, brethren, with what kind of prayer this woman approached our Saviour. It was very earnest, but very simple; she uses no eloquence. no language of persuasion. Her prayer is the cry of a distressed soul for mercy and for help.

There is a very common notion that education is needed to enable a man to pray acceptably. The only education needed is that sought for in the words, 'Lord, teach us to pray,' and the prayers He teaches, be they short ejaculations or long continued supplications, are very plain and simple. 'God be merciful to me a sinner,' 'Lord, that I may receive my sight,' 'Lord, remember me,' 'Lord, thou Son of David, have mercy on me; my daughter is grievously vexed with a devil.'

God needs no eloquent explanation of our wants: no argument but our necessity, no plea but this, that Jesus died for us.

It was, among other reasons, to encourage us in our resort to Him, that God the Son became also the Son of Man, the Man of sorrows and acquainted with grief. This was one reason why He took on Him the experiences of friendship and relationship, of labour and toil, of hunger and thirst, of life and death, that we might come to Him as to One who could enter into and understand our trials and our need, being touched with the feeling of our infirmities, and in all points tempted like as we are, yet without sin. Were the gift of all understanding and of all knowledge yours, could you speak with the tongue of the seraphim, your prayers would not be in the least more worthy of His ear. If His Spirit have taught you to pray, it is the voice of His Spirit in you that He hears; and though your prayers find no expression in words, but consist only of the unuttered groans of a troubled heart, they will surely be heard and answered by Him.

Learn from the prayer of the Canaanite woman a lesson of *perseverance*. Her prayer, at first, brought no sign of any reply from Christ. Then an unfavourable remark, then words which seemed to convey only a reproach. Yet she prayed, and went on praying, till she won the blessing that she sought. How are our few and lifeless prayers, shamed by her steadfast perseverance, especially in our prayers for more grace, for more of the gifts of the Holy Spirit. We are too often content to ask in a cold and formal manner, to ask for them once, or now and then; and if our petitions do not seem to us to be immediately granted, we are tempted to give up the hope of obtaining them, and to pray for them no more. We should scarcely so act if we were seeking mercy and favour from an earthly sovereign. While we request temporal mercies, in submission to the will of Him who best knows what is best for us, let us

## THE CANAANITE MOTHER.          129

seek for spiritual mercies which he has promised to bestow, with *unwavering perseverance*. The door is at times shut against us that we may knock the louder, that by more earnest and oft-repeated prayer we may take the kingdom of heaven, as it were, by violence, and win from our Father, for Jesus' sake, the merciful response, 'Be it unto thee even as thou wilt.' We have in the history before us an exemplary instance of that deep *humility* and conscious *sense* of *unworthiness* with which it becomes sinful and frail man to approach the foot of the throne of God. Apparently rejected and despised, reproached and refused, the sorrowing mother still waits on the Lord Jesus. The indignation of the disciples, the hardest thing that the Lord will say to her or of her, none of these awaken her pride or excite her anger, she accepts them all; content to receive mercy among the vilest, so long as she may but find mercy from Him. Dear brethren, it is fit when we kneel in prayer to remember that had we our deserts from God He would spurn us from His presence, and banish us into outer darkness. May it please Him to open our eyes to see ourselves as we really are in His sight, to show us His holiness and our impurity, His rightful demands and our disobedience, His wisdom and our ignorance, His power and our weakness; that when we pray we may present ourselves

K

before Him in the spirit of this Canaanite, and ask as our Church has taught us: 'We do not presume to come to Thee, O merciful Lord, trusting in our own righteousness, but in Thy manifold and great mercies. We are not worthy so much as to gather up the crumbs under Thy table.'

Lastly, we have in this history an example of *mighty* and *prevailing faith*, that disposition of heart towards God which He has bound Himself never to resist. Place yourselves in her situation, while in deep distress you hear of the arrival of a stranger of Godlike power and might; clothed in a human form. You learn that He has ever shown tenderest compassion for human suffering and necessity. He comes near to your dwelling; you go to meet Him, and cry to Him for help, acknowledging His Divine origin, yet appealing to His human sympathy: 'Have mercy on me, O Lord, thou Son of David.' Instead of the gracious reply you have been led to expect, He turns coldly and silently away.

Resolved not to lose the object of your desire for want of earnestness, you come, even though you hear Him say that He was not sent to such as you. You come and worship Him, and cry, 'Lord, help me.' This time He answers you in words that imply reproach and contempt as well as denial. In such a

## THE CANAANITE MOTHER. 131

case, would not you be tempted to disbelieve all that you had heard of the might and the mercy of Him who could treat you thus? So was she tempted, brethren, yet her faith stood the trial. She had little knowledge in comparison with that which you enjoy. He had not in her day proved Himself to be the Redeemer of mankind by dying for us, and rising again, that every sinful child of Adam's race, whether Jew or Gentile, might come unto Him and have eternal life. But little as was her knowledge, her faith and trust were firm. Her faith was the gift of the Holy Ghost; may the like gift be granted to us, for it has mighty power with God.

Such faith often, by Divine permission, meets with the severest trials; yet is it only so permitted that it may win the most glorious triumph and wear the brightest crown. Of this woman's trial, says Bishop Hall, 'O Saviour, the trial had not been so sharp if Thou hadst not found the faith so strong, if Thou hadst not meant the issue to be so happy. Thou hadst not driven her away as a dog if Thou hadst not intended to admit her for a saint, and to advance her as much for a pattern of faith as Thou depressedst her for a spectacle of contempt.'\* So praying, with like faith, perseverance, and deep humility, let us approach our God in Jesus' name.

\* Bishop Hall's 'Contemplations.'

In such a spirit may we venture to use the language of the Patriarch, 'I will not let Thee go, except Thou bless me;'—assured that the answer shall be—'Be it unto thee, even as thou wilt.'

# XIV.

## REPENTANCE.

### FOR ASH WEDNESDAY.

2 Cor. vii. 10.—'For godly sorrow worketh repentance to salvation not to be repented of: but the sorrow of the world worketh death.'

THESE words correct a very common error on the important subject of repentance. While it is generally supposed that sorrow for sin and repentance are one and the same thing, the text shows us that there may be the first, without any true repentance; and that repentance is not even the same as godly sorrow for sin, but that such godly sorrow works repentance, and is always followed by it. The sorrow here spoken of is of two kinds, sorrow of the world, and godly sorrow, or sorrow according to God. But in each case it is sorrow for sin, as we may see from the rest of the chapter. And as the sorrow itself is twofold, so also are its results. Sorrow of the world worketh spiritual death, while sorrow, according to God, worketh repentance unto salvation not to be repented of. The sorrow of the world worketh death. Sooner or later sin brings its grief to all men, converted or unconverted; all must sorrow for it here or hereafter. Often, very often, unconverted men, men of this world, do even in this life grieve bitterly for past sin. They mourn for it on account of its present consequences. The man whose crimes have brought dishonour on his name, and punishment upon his guilty head; the transgressor whose offences have destroyed every prospect of earthly success; the gambler and the spendthrift ruined; the drunkard as he goes halting along the streets, tied and bound by the sin, once his delight, now his tyrant; the profligate with his body and soul on fire, feeling already a foretaste of eternal woe; the father who never trained his children to fear God above all fear, or to bend their infant knees in prayer in a loving Saviour's name, and who finds the children he trained up in disobedience to God, carrying out his principles in rebellion against himself; think you that these, and others like unto them, do not sorrow for sin? Yet again behold that offender of a more thoughtful class, whose eye is opened upon a dark futurity, over whose portals he sees written lamentation and mourning and woe; chained and sentenced criminal in the prison-house of God's justice; hopeless of escape, because he has no heart for the only Saviour, though he trembles at his coming doom; these all sorrow for sin like him in the Proverbs (v. 11), who mourns at the last, when his flesh and his body are consumed, and says, 'How have I hated instruction, and my heart despised reproof; and have not obeyed the voice of my teachers, nor inclined mine ear to them that instructed me; I was almost in all evil in the midst of the congregation and assembly.' But such sorrow brings no blessing on the mourner's head, no comfort to his comfortless soul. It is not a sorrow according to God, it has no reference to the evil, the ingratitude of sin against Him who alone can give pardon, consolation, and peace, or make the wounded spirit whole. Such mourners, if they could but be set free from the pain they suffer, and the punishment they expect, would plunge deeply and at once into sin again. Their sorrow worketh death. It leads them to consume their days in murmuring against God and bewailing their hard fate, or, if they can, to drink deep of the intoxicating cup of pleasure, and so to drown the misery of the present and the dread of the future; or to occupy their whole souls with the cares of this life, if they may but forget the next, or even to escape the misery of time by self-murder, casting themselves headlong into unutterable and eternal woe. Of such a kind was the sorrow of Cain and of Esau, of Saul, of Ahab, and of Judas. For the sorrow of the world worketh death. Our text mentions another kind of sorrow which St. Paul calls godly sorrow, sorrow which has reference to God, and to the evil of sin, as committed against Him.

Now, concerning this sorrow, note that it by no means excludes grief for those present sufferings which transgression brings upon the sinner, or dread of the threatened judgments of God, and of everlasting condemnation. On the contrary, this grief and dread do enter into all godly sorrow, though, perhaps, most especially into the sorrow of the man who has for the first time been led to see the error of his ways, and to desire to be pardoned and received into favour by the God whom he has so deeply offended. The first feeling that seems to have led to the repentance of the Prodigal Son in the parable, was the feeling of his own misery when he began to be in want, and no man gave unto him: 'I perish for hunger.' But in all true sorrow of this kind there is a regard to God, a sense of sin, and its evil as against a holy Creator and God of perfect purity. The man grieves not only

## REPENTANCE. 137

because he suffers, or dreads future suffering, but because he has rebelled against God. His thoughts turn from his distresses to their cause, and he acknowledges the justice of his pains and fears as he cries, I have sinned against the Lord. Then as God manifests Himself more and more clearly to such a penitent, leading him to see His claims to his service and obedience, showing him the love and gratitude which he owed to Him, giving him to know how hateful sin is in His sight, the man almost loses sight of the consequences of his sin to himself and to others, as prostrate in the dust he exclaims, 'Against Thee, Thee only, have I sinned, and done this evil in Thy sight.' But there is one element in this godly sorrow that we must most carefully keep in sight, and without which it could not exist, and that is, hope in its various degrees producing love to God. No man grieves that he has offended one who has, he thinks, no mercy, no pity for him; but sorrow *according to God*, knows what He really is,—a most merciful and loving Father, Who would not the death of a sinner, but rather that he should be converted and live. What *humble* hope in the breast of the Prodigal shines forth in the first words of godly sorrow that issue from his lips, 'I will arise and go to *my Father*, and will say unto Him, *Father*, I have sinned.' Was there not a trembling hope of mercy in the tears that penitent woman shed when she stood behind the Lord, at His feet, weeping, and washed those feet with tears, and wiped them with the hairs of her head? And then when the Holy Ghost leads the sinner to Calvary, and bids him look upon that sacred, loving face, marred with blows and crowned with thorns, and points him to the agonised and wounded human form stretched out to die, and makes him hear the Saviour's cry of anguish, 'My God, my God, why hast Thou forsaken Me?' when that blest Spirit says by His word applied to the soul, 'O sinner, all this thy Lord did suffer for the love of thee; this *He* bore in *thy* place, that thou shouldest never perish; this cross He endured that thou mightest wear a crown of life and glory eternal; then the hard and stony heart is melted into most true and godly sorrow. As hope rises up towards heaven repentance sinks in deeper self-abasement upon the earth; the penitent, a believer now, hath the eyes of his soul fixed upon his Redeemer! Like St. Peter at the sorrowful yet loving look of his Lord, he weeps bitterly. This is the language of his heart: '*My* sins have crucified Thee, the Lord of glory; *my* wicked hands nailed Thee there. *I* pierced Thy holy heart by my iniquities; yet Thou hast loved me, and given Thyself for me. Now that "mine eye seeth Thee, I abhor myself, and repent in dust and ashes," my Lord and my God.'

This godly sorrow is no transient feeling, no mere sudden flash of emotion, affecting the mind for a few days or hours, and then passing away. As a Christian grows in grace so this sorrow for sin increases in intensity, and penitence becomes the habit of his life. Here on earth he learns more of the love of God from his own experience and from constant communion with Him. He learns more of the holiness of God by the power of the Holy Ghost, enabling him to enter into, and understand the Divine character as displayed in the Scriptures, and exemplified in our Lord's life. By the very practice of holy duty in the strength of that spirit, he comes to feel and comprehend the extent, the beauty, the blessedness of holiness. And at the same time he learns more of the evil of sin. This, from his own experience of its deceitfulness, and of its miserable effect in hindering his communion with God. The love of God in Christ, daily shown to him by the Holy Ghost, kindles and enlivens his own love to God; sin appears to him in all its blackness, as rebellion against love, as a wounding of his Saviour, as grievous to the Holy Ghost the Comforter. Thus the most devout and faithful servant of God, the most earnest lover of his Redeemer, is usually found to have the deepest sorrow for iniquity. This godly sorrow works repentance unto salvation. Repentance being an entire change of mind, heart, and purpose. The aim and end of him who so sorrows for sin is to obtain salvation from sin and its consequences. The burden of sin becomes intolerable to him. He longs to be free from its power dwelling in him. He calls on God the Holy Ghost to enable him to crucify that set of selfish affections, that mass of godless and corrupt imaginations, which once were his delight; sins of which once he thought but little are now his pain and grief, his enemies. He can enter into the spirit of St. Paul's words (Rom. vii. 23, 24), 'But I see another law in my members, warring against the law of my mind, and bringing me into captivity to the law of sin, which is in my members. O wretched man that I am! who shall deliver me from the body of this death?' By grace, his godly sorrow leads him again and again to the fountain opened for sin and for uncleanness. To the atoning work of Christ on the cross he clings more entirely. He has no hope but in Christ, can find no peace but at His feet. From Him freely, from Him alone, he gains salvation from guilt. Through Christ only, he obtains from the Father the Spirit of grace, enabling him to fight the good fight of faith, and gain many a victory. Thus he expects that in the end, he, with all believers, shall be completely freed from the power of sin, and be made more than conquerors through Him that loved them.

'Salvation not to be repented of.' How many earthly objects we have won by earnest struggles, that have proved vain and empty, or, it may be, exceeding bitter to us when we gained them. How have we deplored the toil and pains we lavished to procure them! But this salvation, who that has tasted, repents of it! What Christian repents him of his prayers, and tears and efforts? Who ever repented that he had found the Lord, crucified for him, and received the grant of salvation with its accompaniments of grace from His loving hand? And there, where the noble army of martyrs awaits the last addition to its ranks, there, where are those that came out of great tribulation and washed their robes in the blood of the Lamb, where they hold the harps of God, and bear in their hands the palms of victory; in all that countless multitude, is there one that repents him of the salvation he hath won? Ask them; it is with one loud voice that they reply, 'Salvation unto our God which sitteth upon the throne, and unto the Lamb!'

## XV.

### THE ABSENT LORD WATCHING OVER HIS CHURCH.

#### FOR ASCENSION DAY.

St. Mark, vi., first part verse 48.—'He saw them toiling in rowing.'

HE saw *them*, but they saw not *Him*. For a time He was hidden from their eyes; to all appearance they were left in darkness and weariness and difficulty, to row their wave-beaten boat to shore as best they might. They were learning the hardest of all lessons; they were learning to obey an unseen Lord, to trust in strength and support invisible—save to the eye of faith—a lesson rendered necessary by the fall. It is not in man's nature to walk by faith; God did not create man to walk by faith; Adam was created to enjoy the sight of his Maker, so far as a created being could bear the sight. God the Son, the Eternal Word, was probably pleased to reveal Himself to Adam frequently, as He did afterwards on three occasions to the patriarchs, in human form. God spoke to him face to face, and Adam heard, and was not afraid. But when by disobedience he rebelled, Adam lost this privilege. He was driven out from Eden, and from the presence of the Lord. Defiled and unclean, he was no longer fit to enjoy that intercourse with God for which he was at first created. Now, he needed to have his sins expiated, and put away; and not only so, it now became necessary that his nature should be changed, his heart and mind renewed, the image of God restored in him. He now had to be trained anew in the habit and practice of that obedience which he had renounced. He was now unholy, and must be made holy ere he could be admitted to the visible presence of his Creator. Through toil, and pain, and chastisement, through the grave and gate of death he must pass, as his training for immortality and for the unclouded presence of his Lord. He must walk awhile by faith, that he may be prepared, and that for ever, to walk by sight. When that process is over, and that probation complete, then, and not till then, will the highest desires of our nature be satisfied. Then, in His presence, the redeemed will find fulness of joy, and at his right hand pleasures for evermore (Psalm xvi. 11).

Too often, brethren, nature revolts from this,

and refuses to submit to this training. Man would fain enter at once upon the joys and privileges of sight. If he may not behold his God, he will adopt some visible substitute or representation in His place. To this rebellious desire, we must ascribe the golden calves of the Israelite, the idols of the heathen, the images of the Romanist. To this, the unscriptural doctrine of a real presence of Christ's natural flesh and blood in the Holy Communion,\* a doctrine which involves, as the Church declares, idolatry —to be abhorred of all faithful Christians.

This hard lesson of obedience to and trust in an unseen Saviour the Apostles were beginning to learn, as they toiled in rowing upon the storm-tossed lake of Galilee.

Now, let us turn to the other side of the picture. They were not favoured with His outward presence, even though their trial was brought upon them through simple obedience to His commands.

But look up at the mountain-side over against the lake.—Who is that alone in prayer,—alone with the Father? It is their Lord; and can we doubt that He is praying for them? Mark his steadfast gaze directed towards the lake. They saw Him not; yet

\* For the Sacramental bread and wine remain still in their very natural substances.—*Black Rubric.* (ED.)

His eye was upon them — 'He saw them toiling in rowing.' He beheld their obedience. He sympathised with their weary toil, and when they were ready to faint He stood by them. No apparent impossibility could hinder His coming to them. No waves or storms could obstruct His passage, when He was satisfied with the proof of their obedience. He went unto them, walking on the sea; and the trial was over, and the wind ceased, and soon they reached in safety the shore whither they were bound.

The Apostles at this time were, probably, not fully convinced of the great truth that their Master was God as well as man. They were not aware that His eye was the eye of Omniscience. They doubted not that He had a right to command, and that it was their duty to obey. But what comfort and encouragement would they have enjoyed that night, had they known that He was One Whose almighty arm could reach them across the waves; from Whom neither night nor distance could hide them; that the darkness was no darkness to Him; that He was waiting to save them; and that in their most pressing necessity He would deliver them. This was the sacred part of the lesson that they were to learn from that Divine interference. Thus were they being prepared for the time when He should be finally taken from them into heaven;

when they must walk the rest of their life-journey by faith, and obey, and suffer, and die, trusting in One they could not see. They were to be assured that He was watching over them with the eye that slumbereth not; that He would be ever ready to interpose on their behalf, and to vouchsafe His grace and help, just in their hour of sorest need. That hour soon arrived. The day came, when having died for man's sin, and risen again for the justification of all that would believe on Him, He was taken up from them into heaven, as He blessed them. With mingled feelings of painful longing, and triumphant joy and wonder, they stood gazing up at That solitary figure rising solemnly in the air, until the cloud enfolded Him, and received Him from their sight. Then, by the words of angels, they were taught no longer to expect His visible presence with His Church, but to look onward, in faith and hope, to His second advent in glory, when He shall come again, and receive His people to Himself; and so shall they be ever with the Lord. 'Ye men of Galilee, why stand ye gazing up into heaven? this same Jesus, which is taken from you into heaven, shall so come in like manner as ye have seen Him go into heaven.' (Acts, i. 11.) 'He ascended into heaven, and sitteth on the right hand of God the Father Almighty.'

My brethren, our Lord has gone up into a mountain apart, to the heavenly Zion, God's holy hill, golden Jerusalem. There, at the right hand of God, He ever liveth, to make intercession for us. Thence, He sees us as we toil and row in His ship, the Church, on our voyage to the haven of everlasting rest. Thence, in every time of need, He sends to us from the Father, the Spirit of wisdom and comfort and sanctity and power. The Holy Ghost renews our failing strength, and refreshes our fainting hearts, and keeps us from falling before temptation. He does more, He purifies our spirit; He guides us with His holy counsel, until our Lord shall come again, not as once before, walking on the waters, but with trumpets' blasts, enthroned upon the clouds of heaven, with angel hosts attending, and surrounded by His saints. Now, our cry to him must be,—

> 'Thou art gone up on high,
> To mansions in the sky;
> And round Thy throne unceasingly,
> The songs of praise arise;
> But we are lingering here,
> With sin and care oppressed;
> Lord, send Thy promised Comforter,
> And lead us to Thy rest.'

Our onward journey is to be one of 'toiling

in rowing.' But, as regards spiritual matters, so long as we are not in earnest, we are comparatively at our ease. It is not till our eyes are opened to the exceeding sinfulness of sin, the danger of indifference, the horrors of a lost eternity, that we seek to know what keeps us from Christ for salvation, or from preparing to dwell for ever in His presence.

It is then that Satan rises up against us, by force to drive us back, or by craft to turn us aside, from the right way. It is no easy thing to walk as seeing Him who is invisible, to live consistently, and persistently to endure to the end. You need both His Spirit and His own spiritual presence for this. Let the thought that He sees your striving, encourage you to ask these blessings. You, who are toiling in resistance to temptation, in the crucifixion of some besetting sin, some wicked passion, some ungodly temper, some wretched fear of man, and man's opinion,—you, toilers in your Saviour's service, Christians who work diligently for your own support and that of your families,—you who labour under any form of persecution or enmity, for Christ's sake,—you who may have to endure sickness and sorrow and disappointment, who will probably have to toil and struggle for breath upon a dying bed,—Oh, what if you are Christ's?

Then, He sees you toiling, He understands your difficulties better than you do yourselves. Your ascended Lord is all the while interceding for you, offering your cries for grace and help, with the sweet incense of His own most precious blood and perfect righteousness; and He will send to you from the Father the Holy Ghost, that He may abide with you for ever. Remember and be encouraged by the remembrance, for Him the Father heareth always.

Finally, I have to remind you that while you are engaged toiling in obedience to His commands, He Himself will draw near, and go with you. His bodily presence is indeed in heaven. He will not come to you, therefore, as He came to His disciples, walking on the sea, yet 'He will not leave you comfortless;' 'He will come to you.' He will manifest Himself to you as He does not to the world. His own words are, 'He that hath My commandments, and keepeth them, he it is that loveth Me, and he that loveth Me shall be loved of My Father; and I will love him and manifest Myself unto him;' and again, 'If a man love Me, he will keep My words; and My Father will love him, and We will come to him, and make Our abode with him.' (St. John, xiv. 21–23.)

This manifestation of Himself by Christ to His servants is no mere form of speech. His promises are no mere empty words of encouragement. He comes to them, so that they know His presence and feel its effects. Their hearts burn within them as He stands by them while they are praying, or makes Himself known to them in the breaking of bread at the Holy Communion,—as He shines on them in the darkness of toil and suffering, or brightens with His company the chamber of death.

Paul and Silas felt His presence in the dungeon, and sang their midnight hymn of joy and praise.

'I have peace deep as a river. Jesus does all things well,' wrote a dying officer on the field of battle, when his mouth was shot away, and he could not speak. The Lord was with him, manifesting His presence then. I have seen the dying eye light up with glory as the trembling lips pronounced the name of One who was there manifested, though I saw Him not.

My brethren, He sees His disciples toiling in rowing, and nothing can keep Him from them in their hour of need. He is watching them now from the mountain whither he has gone up again to pray. But the time is at hand when His intercession will be over, and His long watch ended, and He shall come again to be our Judge.

Oh, Christian people, watch you now and pray, that on that awful day you may be placed at His right hand, and numbered with His saints in glory everlasting.

## XVI.

PRAYER FOR THE HOLY GHOST.

FOR WHITSUNDAY.

Num. xx. 8.—'Take the rod, and gather thou the assembly together, thou, and Aaron thy brother, and speak ye unto the rock before their eyes: and it shall give forth his water, and thou shalt bring forth to them water out of the rock.'

THE history of which the text is a part has many circumstances of resemblance to that which is told in Exodus xvii., while in some points there is a remarkable difference between them. From the resemblance, indeed, the same name was given to each place; they were both called Meribah, strife or contention, because of the rebellious strife of the people with the Lord who had brought them out of the land of Egypt. But this sameness of name must not mislead us into supposing that the transactions were the same. In the first instance, as the children of

Israel were on their journey from Egypt to Sinai, where the Law was to be given, they came, we are told, to Rephidim, where there was no water for the people to drink. Instead of praying for relief, 'the people did chide with Moses, and said, Give us water that we may drink. And Moses said unto them, Why chide ye with me? wherefore do ye tempt the Lord? And the people thirsted there for water; and the people murmured against Moses, and said, Wherefore is this that thou hast brought us up out of Egypt to kill us, and our children, and our cattle with thirst? And Moses cried unto the Lord, saying, What shall I do unto this people? they be almost ready to stone me. And the Lord said unto Moses, Go on before the people, and take with thee of the elders of Israel; and thy rod, wherewith thou smotest the river, take in thine hand, and go. Behold, I will stand before thee there upon the rock in Horeb: and thou shalt smite the rock, and there shall come water out of it that the people may drink. And Moses did so in the sight of the elders of Israel. And he called the name of the place Massah and Meribah, because of the chiding of the children of Israel.' (Exod. xvii. 2–7.)

In this account there is one thing to which I would especially direct your attention, and that is, that God would stand upon the rock, and *then*

Moses was commanded to smite the rock, which being smitten they were supplied with water both then and afterwards.\* For St. Paul tells us 'they drank of that spiritual Rock that followed them, and that Rock was (*i. e.* meant) Christ.' (1 Cor. x. 4.) There seems no scriptural ground for the idea that the stream from this very rock that was smitten followed them in their journeys. It is far more probable that wherever they wandered in that mountainous desert a rock typical of Christ poured forth its water for them in fresh supplies. There came, however, a time when, in the providence of God, the stream ceased to flow. Probably for the trial of their trust in God, Who had so long supplied their need. In Num. xx. 2, we read of the ungrateful, unbelieving murmurs of the Israelites: 'And there was no water for the congregation : and they gathered together against Moses and against Aaron. And the people chode with Moses, and spake, saying, Would God that we had died when our brethren died before the Lord ! And why have ye brought up the congregation of the Lord into this wilderness, that we and our cattle should die there ? And wherefore have ye made us to

---

\* 'As there were *clouds* wherever they went from which the manna fell, so likewise there were rocks from which the waters flowed.'— *Wordsworth in loc.*

come up out of Egypt, to bring us unto this evil place ? It is no place of seed, or of figs, or of vines, or of pomegranates; neither is there any water to drink.' In the text we have the command of God on that occasion : 'Take the rod, and gather thou the assembly together, thou and Aaron thy brother, and speak ye unto the rock before their eyes; and it shall give forth his water, and thou shalt bring forth to them water out of the rock.' And in vers. 10–12 we read of the disobedience of Moses, and of the great wrath of God, although, in pity to a perishing multitude, He did not withhold from them a supply of water. 'And Moses and Aaron gathered the congregation together before the rock, and he said unto them, Hear now, ye rebels; must we fetch you water out of this rock ? And Moses lifted up his hand, and with his rod he smote the rock twice; and the water came out abundantly, and the congregation drank, and their beasts also. And the Lord spake unto Moses and Aaron, Because ye believed me not, to sanctify me in the eyes of the children of Israel, therefore ye shall not bring this congregation into the land which I have given them.'

These things are types, true as histories. They are written to teach us not only the sin of murmuring against God in our hour of trial, but also higher and more deeply spiritual lessons. And to those I desire, in reliance on the power of the Holy Ghost, to lead your minds on this high festival of the Church.

The Rock whence the water flowed is declared by St. Paul to have been an emblem of Christ. 1 Cor. x. 4 : ' And did all drink the same spiritual drink : for they drank of that spiritual Rock that followed them, and that Rock was Christ.' The same comparison is used in other places in Holy Scripture. He is the ' Rock of our refuge' (Ps. xciv. 22) ; 'the Rock of our salvation' (Ps. xcv. 1); the Rock of ages (Isa. xxvi. 4); for such, as you will see in the margin, is the original expression translated ' everlasting strength.' This Rock was smitten for us on the cross. It was needful that it should be so. He was there ' wounded for our transgressions. He was bruised for our iniquities : the chastisement of our peace was upon Him, and with His stripes we are healed.' (Isa. liii. 5.) From His wounded side His smitten frame poured forth the blood of atonement and the water of purification. It was needful that the blood should be shed, in order that, our guilt being put away, we might receive from the Father the Holy Spirit. He was needed to cleanse our hearts from the love and power of sin, to restore in us our Creator's image, and to fit us for His presence. The water that poured forth from the smitten rock was a type of the Holy Ghost on the day of Pentecost, the first great Whitsuntide, sent by Christ from the Father. Of that Holy Ghost inwardly poured forth on every servant of God from first to last; following the Lord's host, the Church militant, as guided by the Captain of their salvation through the wilderness towards their eternal home; supplying every need of their souls, according to the promise in St. John, xiv. 16, 17: 'And I will pray the Father, and He shall give you another Comforter, that He may abide with you for ever; even the Spirit of truth. Whom the world cannot receive, because it seeth Him not, neither knoweth Him : but ye know Him, for He dwelleth with you, and shall be in you.'

This use of water as a type of the Holy Spirit pervades the whole of Scripture. This blessed Spirit is the water spoken of by Ezekiel (xxxvi. 25, 26): 'Then will I sprinkle clean water upon you, and ye shall be clean : from all your filthiness and from all your idols will I cleanse you. A new heart also will I give you, and a new spirit will I put within you; and I will take away the stony heart out of your flesh, and I will give you an heart of flesh.' He is the water promised by our Lord (St. John, vii. 38, 39): 'He that believeth on Me, as the Scripture hath said, out of his belly shall flow rivers of living water. But this spake He of the Spirit, which they that believe on Him should receive; for the Holy Ghost was not yet given, because that Jesus was not yet glorified.' He is the living water shown to St. John (Rev. xxii. 1): 'And He showed me a pure river of water of life, clear as crystal, proceeding out of the throne of God and of the Lamb.'

From this subject, brethren, learn—

I. What is the great need of the Church of God. The Israelites had a perfect organization, a Divine government, abundance of flocks and herds, and they were many in number, an immense army for mutual protection and defence. But one thing they had not; without it all the rest were of no avail; for want of it they were stayed on their journey to the promised land. Except this want had been supplied, as a nation and as individuals they must have perished; a desert strewn with skeletons must have been a monument of their sins, and a token that God had forsaken them.

Just so is it with the Christian Church. It may enjoy, as does our own, a magnificent organization, in which each minister and each member has his own work and place and privileges. It may be in the eyes of the enemy terrible as an army with banners, awful as the camp of Israel, seen nightly from the mountains of Moab. How peacefully it lay around its Tabernacle, at rest and fearless because above, suspended in the air, hung that mysterious column of fire—sign that the Lord of hosts was there! The Church may enjoy a divinely sanctioned ministry of Bishops, Priests, and Deacons, and her members may be as the sand which is by the seashore for multitude. Yet all this will be of no avail, if the flowing of the pure river of water of life be withheld from us by God, if the Holy Ghost be not given. If Christian people be deficient as a body in zeal for the faith and in holiness, in unity amongst themselves, in love for the souls of unbelievers, in soberness of spirit, and in self-denial,—if errors, and divisions, and heresies have sprung up amongst them, —brethren, it is for want of a larger stream of the grace of the Holy Ghost pouring forth from Him once smitten at Calvary, but now our risen and ascended Lord.

And as it is with the Church, so with every member thereof. Without deep draughts of His grace who can hold fast by faith in Christ? who can live a Christlike life, preserving a holy consistency in the midst of a tempting world? Have you ever tried to pray one real prayer without Him; to kill one evil lust or passion; to love your God and your Redeemer; to gain a blessing from the word and sacraments; or to convey a blessing to others? If you have, let your failure bring you to confess that without this living water your souls are dead, helpless, and unclean. As water to the body, so a supply of this living water to the soul is the great necessity for life's sustenance. Learn,

II. That, in order to obtain this promised gift, Christ is not to be offered over again. Herein consisted one great cause of offence given by Moses and shared in, no doubt, by Aaron (ver. 11). The rock, once smitten, was to be smitten no more. 'Christ, being raised from the dead, dieth no more,' says the word of God; 'death hath no more dominion over Him.' (Rom. vi. 9.) And again, 'This Man, after He had offered one sacrifice for sins for ever, sat down on the right hand of God.' (Heb. x. 12.) And our Church teaches the same, saying that on the cross He made by His one offering of Himself, *once* offered, a full, perfect, and sufficient sacrifice, oblation, and satisfaction for the sins of the whole world. Among her many deadly errors this is a conspicuous error of the Church of Rome and of all such in our own or any other branch of Christ's visible Church as follow Romish doctrine, that they would in effect, if not in form, *smite the Rock* as often as they would call forth living water from on high; they would offer up Christ again and again as the purchase of fresh supplies of the grace of the Holy Ghost. No priest hath power to lay Christ upon the altar and offer Him now to God. The only sacrifice that we can offer to God in the Holy Communion, or at any other time, is, as says our Church, following Holy Scripture (Rom. xii. 1), the sacrifice of ourselves unto Him, and of our praise and thanksgiving: 'Offer unto God thanksgiving: and pay thy vows unto the Most High.' (Ps. l. 14.)

III. In order to bring down living water from the Rock, that Rock once smitten must now be spoken to; we now win by prayer from Christ that which He died upon the cross to win for us.

My brethren, would you drink of that water of which he who partakes shall thirst no more for the low pleasures and fading profits of the world? Would you drink of that water which springeth up in them that drink it unto everlasting life? Would you have in you that Holy Ghost whose presence is an earnest of your inheritance, a pledge that heaven, with all its blessings, is yours? Speak to the Rock; plead in prayer with the King of glory. There are times in the history of the Church, and times in the life of every Christian, when the grace of the Holy Spirit seems at least to be withheld, as the water from the rock was for a while withdrawn at this second Meribah. When the work of the Church languishes, and the enemy comes in like a flood, and the love of many waxes cold; when the Christian feels as if left alone to fight the good fight, and begins to faint in his heavenward journey; faith is weak, and love grows cold, and temptation is powerful. Such times are overruled and permitted of God, to show us what we are when left to ourselves, what we are when left without the abundance of His grace. At such times especially, as well as at all others, let us be very earnest in prayer for Almighty grace. God is at such times leading us to the Rock, calling us into closer communion with Himself. Let us then in public pray most heartily, 'We beseech Thee leave us not comfortless, but send to us Thine Holy Ghost.' And in private let us cry mightily to Christ that He would plead with the Father for a renewed pouring forth of that blessed Spirit's grace on all around us and on ourselves. Speak ye unto the Rock, and it shall give forth His water. 'If ye, being evil, know how to give good gifts unto your children, how much more shall your heavenly Father give the Holy Spirit to them that ask Him?'

## XVII.

### MEMORY, AND THE WORK OF THE HOLY GHOST THEREON.

#### FOR WHITSUNDAY.

St. John, xiv. 26.—'But the Comforter, which is the Holy Ghost, whom the Father will send in my name, He shall teach you all things, and bring all things to your remembrance, whatsoever I have said unto you.'

IT is to the consideration of the latter part of the text, brethren, that I desire to lead your attention at present. He shall bring all 'things to your remembrance, whatsoever I have said unto you;' and I think it may not be out of place if I say a few words first about that wonderful faculty which is alluded to in the text, the faculty or power of memory. It is not a power or attribute of God; we cannot, strictly speaking, say that God remembers or forgets, for God not only sees all things, but sees them all, past, present, and future, *at once*. He sees them *all always*. When we call on God the Father to remember or forget, as we are taught to do in Holy Scripture, we are only using language suited to our understandings, and entreating Him to look on us with favour or forgiveness as to those doings or sayings of ours which are always in His sight. But the power of memory is one which God has given to man. We cannot, as *He* can, see everything, past and present, in a moment. So He has given us the power of calling back to our minds things that are long gone by, the power of hearing them again, or of seeing them brought before us, as it were, in a picture. This is a very great, in some respects an awful power. It has a great deal to do with our happiness or misery on earth, a great deal to do with the happiness of heaven, and it will form a great part of the misery of hell. If I were to ask you what you were doing now, you would most of you say, we are living our daily lives, and doing our day's work in that state to which it has pleased God to call us. Very true; but, brethren, we are also doing something else that we are apt to forget; we are painting pictures for memory, pictures not easily blotted out. That which we say or do will come back again to our minds, often upon earth while we live, in the hour of death, and in the day of judgment, and in eternity. How bitter the sight of some of these pictures is, and will be. even upon earth, especially when it is too late to add pictures of a happier kind. How many a one has for life to see in his thoughts a picture of himself, a cruel son to a suffering and helpless parent, a brutal husband to an unoffending wife, a wretched example to his unoffending children. And, O brethren, when death steps in and fixes the picture so that no tears, no change of conduct, can make amends to them that are gone to their long home, what a curse does memory become, how agonising the sights which it brings before our view! Happy if those pictures be by faith in Jesus, and repentance before God, blotted out in the blood of the Lamb, ere it be too late and repentance be impossible. and eternal remorse begun. Think of those solemn words in St. Luke, xvi. 25—'Son. remember.' Think of the picture ever before his eyes. He sees a noble mansion, by the stately door of which lies a patient, suffering. child of God, neglected and despised, contented if he may be fed with a few of the crumbs that fall from the loaded table within; his eye passes on to the inner chambers, there he sees a proud and luxurious man, splendidly clothed, and faring sumptuously every day, enjoying God's gifts. but showing no gratitude to the Giver, never kneeling in prayer, never weeping in penitence, never looking up with faith and love to God. A man gratifying every wish of his wicked heart, setting that heart upon earthly goods, so that they become *his* good things, the only good things he cares for;—living *for himself*—so long, that at length all is over and he dies *to himself*. And now, not a drop of water to cool his burning tongue! And at those words, 'Son, remember.' he lifts up his eyes, being in torments, and *that* is the picture he beholds; and he knows that *that* man is himself, that he, who might have been saved, but would not, is *himself*, now suffering the pain of everlasting fire! O brethren, take care what pictures you are painting, the pictures of your lives. The walls of hell are hung round with them. Even now much is past that we would gladly recall, but cannot. Thank God that though the pain of memory must remain while we live, yet the bitterest sting thereof, the guilt in the sight of God, is taken away from them that have sought and obtained mercy at the cross of Jesus, when the Lord did lay upon Him the iniquity of us all. My brethren, since we all possess this wonderful power of memory, let it be impressed upon our minds that we should strive to make our remembrances pleasant and profitable things. You who are unconverted, while yet the sword of vengeance is kept from falling upon your heads, while God is patient, and holds out the golden sceptre of His mercy, that you may touch it and find pardon there, strive and pray that you may be able henceforth to *remember* that you sinned deeply indeed, but that Jesus died for *you*, that you believed in Him and were forgiven, justified, adopted into the family of heaven, made heirs of God, and joint heirs with Christ. What a memory that will be for a dying bed, what a blessed, holy, and happy memory for eternity! And you, my Christian brethren, who by grace are trying to act up to your baptismal vow, let not the pictures you are painting for memory be such as it will grieve you to look upon when you come to die. There are such pictures, seen even by the dying believer. He can say sometimes, I believe that I am pardoned for my Saviour's sake; but I see a picture of a Christian man drawing tightly his purse-strings when called on to give for Jesus' sake, and that man *had it* to give, and that grudging one was *myself.* I see the likeness of a Christian man who would not go out of his way for an hour to hear of the work of his Master's servants among Jews, Mahometans, and Heathens, and that man was *myself.* I see the picture of a Christian man too often from false shame trying to hide his Christian profession symbolised by the baptismal cross upon his brow—that timid Christian was *myself!* Rather let each of us seek grace so to live that when we come to die we may be enabled to say, 'I look back upon memory's picture of the past, and I see a soldier and servant of Christ crucified, who was enabled by the Holy Ghost to fight the good fight, and to be more than conqueror through Him that loved him; who, in the midst of much sinfulness and infirmity, yet was enabled to labour and deny himself, and to have patience for his Saviour's sake, and that soldier of the cross, that servant of the Lord, was *myself!* The time of my departure is at hand, I am altogether unworthy; my best doings could only be accepted when cleansed from their sinfulness by the blood of Christ; yet in the strength of His Spirit I tried to do what I could for the love of Him, and henceforth there is laid up for me a crown of glory, which the Lord the righteous Judge shall give me in that day. To help us so to live, that our life may present to our memory such a picture on our dying day the promise in the text is given. 'He shall bring all things to your remembrance, whatsoever I have said unto you.'

This promise of the Holy Ghost had, no doubt, a primary and most important reference to the work of writing the New Testament, committed to the Apostles and disciples of the Lord. According to this promise that work was inspired by the Holy Ghost. Does it excite our wonder to see how the Evangelists recorded the very words of the Lord Jesus at such length, so fully and minutely,—to note how one Evangelist writes those very things which others leave out so as to make up one complete and glorious Gospel? Does the infidel object that it was impossible for them so to call to mind the sayings of our Lord? *We* know that to natural power of memory it was impossible. We believe that things which are impossible with men are possible with God; and we are sure that, when these men wrote the Gospel, the promise in the text was fulfilled, that the Holy Ghost did bring to their remembrance all things whatsoever Jesus had said unto them, and that they 'wrote as they were moved' by Him.

But the prophecy or promise in the text has yet, brethren, a further reference, and its blessings reach even to ourselves. To us who believe, it is said, 'He shall bring all things to your remembrance, whatsoever I have said unto you.' Mark the word, remind or bring to your remembrance. Our Lord does not say *reveal*. The promise is not that the Holy Ghost shall speak to the souls of men, and tell them who have neglected to hear or read the words of

Christ, words that they have never heard before, but that 'He shall bring to your remembrance' the things which Christ has spoken to you; and He speaks to you now by His Holy Word. To this would I crave your most deep, reverent, and prayerful attention. I beg you, as you value your hope of salvation, not to neglect these title-deeds of an heavenly inheritance; read, mark, learn, and think upon them inwardly at home; listen earnestly to the Lessons, Gospel, and Epistle in Church; try to recall them when you are alone; let the word of Christ be laid up in your minds as in a store-house, and let that word 'dwell in you richly in all wisdom' (Col. iii. 16). Then pray God for Jesus' sake to grant you the promise in the text, and you will find, not only that the Holy Ghost will bring 'to your remembrance whatsoever things Christ has said to you,' but that He will bring to your memory just such of the Saviour's words as suit your case, and just at the time when you need them most.

See from Holy Scripture how He does this. To strengthen our faith in Christ when any of the declarations of the Saviour are fulfilled, the Holy Ghost reminds us that so Christ hath declared long before. Do we meet with trials in our Christian course? He brings to our minds (St. John, xvi. 33). 'These things I have spoken unto you, that in Me ye might have peace. In the world ye shall have tribulation: but be of good cheer; I have overcome the world.' Or perhaps in time of persecution, He puts it into the heart of one of His servants to bring it to our remembrance, which is the same thing as in Acts, xiv. 21–22, 'And when they had preached the Gospel to that city, and had taught many, they returned again to Lystra, and to Iconium, and Antioch, Confirming the souls of the disciples, and exhorting them to continue in the faith, and that we must through much tribulation enter into the kingdom of God;' that so our confidence may be reassured, and we may be persuaded that trials come, not by chance, but as foreordained for our own good by our Father, and foretold by our Saviour. Take another instance in St. John, ii. 22: 'When therefore He was risen from the dead, His disciples remembered that He had said this unto them; and they believed the Scripture and the word which Jesus had said.' So that the faith of the disciples was confirmed in the Divine foreknowledge of their Lord and Saviour.

Do we need guidance in doubtful circumstances? He brings to our remembrance the words of the Lord Jesus (Acts, xi. 16): 'Then remembered I the word of the Lord, how that

He said, John indeed baptized with water; but ye shall be baptized with the Holy Ghost.' And so St. Peter was guided to do that about which he was at first uncertain, and to receive the first-fruits of the Gentiles into the Church of Christ. How often does the Christian need to be stirred up to duty, to self-denial, to laborious effort for His dear name's sake, and how often does the Holy Ghost bring to his mind some of the tender, solemn exhortations of his Lord, who bought him with His blood. So He did to the elders (or, as we translate the word in our Prayer-book, priests) of the Church at Ephesus by the lips of St. Paul (Acts, xx. 35): 'I have showed you all things, how that so labouring ye ought to support the weak, and to remember the words of the Lord Jesus, how He said, It is more blessed to give than to receive.'

Once more when, through want of prayer and watchfulness, through strong temptation, through pride and self-confidence, a Christian has been betrayed into sin, then the loving Spirit of God brings him to repentance by recalling to his mind the words of Him who for his sake endured the scourge and the thorns, and all the agonies of the passion. This He did for St. Peter when he had denied his Lord, blessing to his memory that loving, sorrowing, look of Jesus, so that (St. Matt. xxvi. 75) 'He went out and wept bitterly.' Brethren, may the Holy Spirit so vouchsafe to sanctify our memory, reminding us according to our hourly need of the words of Jesus, enabling us to shape our life's course by those blessed words, that when we lie a dying our dying memories may be happy memories, and that at the great day we may render up our account with joy, and not with grief.

## XVIII.

### STEWARDSHIP.

St. Luke, xvi., last clause of ver. 2.—'Give an account of thy stewardship; for thou mayest be no longer steward.'

THERE is a word in this passage unexpected by the greater number of those who will hear it one day,—God only knows how soon,—a word the meaning of which, unless we be first taught it by the Holy Ghost, will shine out in characters of fire on our affrighted souls in the judgment time! Conscience, no longer blinded by things seen and by the god of this world, will then awake to the truth,—will behold things as they really are, or, as it will at that day be expressed, as they really *were*. That word is *Stewardship*. Let me try to speak that which most men think; you shall judge whether I state their opinions fairly or no.

I possess a fair property, says one; I hold a good position in society, I enjoy the esteem and respect of friends and neighbours; I have influence in the world, life, and health, and strength. I cannot tell how long I may have these things, but so long as I have them they are fairly mine to use them and to enjoy them as I will, if I do not abuse them for sinful purposes. They are my own. 'Give an account of thy stewardship; for thou mayest be no longer steward!'

I have a fair education, says another, some talents carefully cultivated, much general knowledge that renders my conversation attractive. I have acquired and improved these gifts with toil and pains; they are fairly mine,—I may employ them as it pleases me and wrong no one. Again from heaven the call, 'Give an account of thy stewardship; for thou mayest be no longer steward!'

I have leisure, says a third; I have no occasion to work for my bread; my hours, and days, and weeks are at my disposal. I have in all probability abundance of time before me, and my time is my own.

And I, adds yet another, I am a poor man; I have little, very little I can call my own; some strength, some skill, a few friends, a very little time of leisure, a very little money. I work very hard for all I have; I earn it, and I do think I may fairly call it mine. Yet there rings forth the answer, like the tolling of a death-knell, 'Give an account of thy stewardship; for thou mayest be no longer steward!'

Can this be true? This word 'steward' sounds strangely in our ears. We are aware that all we have comes from God in one sense, yet surely He has made it over to us; surely it is ours? So men say—so, for the most part, they think: but the Lord of all, the Judge before whose tribunal quick and dead must stand, He takes a very different view of the subject; in His eyes all we have is but a loan entrusted to our care for a certain purpose and for a limited time. We are but servants and not masters,—stewards and not proprietors. And of all we have and are there must be strict reckoning. 'Give an account of thy stewardship; for thou mayest be no longer steward.' Life is a stewardship; the living man a steward.

Brethren, how many Christians are defective in their estimate of their position and its duties as viewed in the light of our text. And yet this is the view set before us in Holy Scripture, and with especial distinctness in the New Testament. Christian people are servants; to them are entrusted *talents* (St. Matt. xxv. 14), to be so improved that at the coming of the Master He may receive His own with usury; servants, or slaves, to whom are entrusted, according to another parable, *pounds* (St. Luke, xix. 12), with the charge, 'Occupy till I come.' The ministers of religion, if striving to do their duty, are described by our Lord as faithful and wise stewards (St. Luke, xii. 42). They are husbandmen to whom the vineyard is let, and from whom the Lord expects a return of the fruit of the vineyard. (St. Luke, xx. 9.)

Here I may be met by the reply. All this is nothing new to us, we all confess it; all we have is God's, and it is our duty to employ a portion of it in His service and for His glory.

Now, brethren, that which I desire to impress upon you is, that it is our duty to employ *all* in His service and for His glory. Take those passages in which Christians are spoken of as servants, stewards, and husbandmen. Take them alone, and the modified view so generally held may seem to be the true one. But no passage of Holy Scripture is to be interpreted without reference to the rest of the word of God. You must view these texts in the light of such language as this, 'Ye are not your own, ye are bought with a price; therefore glorify God in your body, and in your spirit, which are God's.' (1 Cor. vi. 20.) A purchased slave can hold no property of his own; all that he has is his master's, and is to be spent in his service. And what if the slave has in matchless mercy been enfranchised — nay more, adopted into his master's family, and made a child of God, an heir of God, a joint-heir with Christ? Surely this does but add to the obligation under which the Christian lies. He must be faithful in his stewardship; he must regard himself, and all that he has, as not his own, but his Father's,— as something for which he must account, when the only-begotten Son shall return and demand a reckoning from each member of His Father's family. Ye are stewards. 'Whether, therefore, ye eat or drink, or whatsoever ye do, do all to the glory of God.' (1 Cor. x. 31.)

This, brethren, is the rule, the law of our stewardship, and what a picture of happiness and beauty does it set before us!—a son in his father's household, entrusted by that father with a portion of his goods. Full of love to his father, bent upon doing his father's will, and promoting his father's glory, earnestly desiring the peace and well-being of every member of the family, making these things his great end in life, and studying to further them by every means in his power; holding all he has as a trust, not a gift, ever mindful that for all he must give account. If we by grace were striving to live by this rule, what carefulness would it work in us; yea, what clearing of ourselves from earth's entanglements; yea, what indignation against sin; yea, what fear of offending; yea, what vehement desire for the abiding presence of the Holy Ghost; yea, what zeal for our Father's service; yea, what revenge against our sinful selves! But how little do even the best Christians among us act up to the rule here given! A little time, a little effort, a little strength, a little money for God, and all the rest for self! And here is the peril, that we think *much* of that *little*, and *little of all* that we devote to ourselves. We are apt to be well content because *we* do something, while *many* do nothing.

Brethren, what I desire for you and for myself, what I pray for on behalf of all, is this— that we may never be addressed by our Lord in those terrible words, 'How is it that I hear this of thee?' Thank God for everything, even trial and disappointment, even sickness and weakness, that brings to our minds, and impresses on our memory, our stewardship and its approaching close—the day when we shall be summoned to 'give an account' of it, 'for thou mayest be no longer steward.' Does it seem to any of us a hard saying; is this to *nature* a burdensome service? I grant it and feel it. But then *nature* must be conquered, and every thought brought into obedience to Christ. And there is only one way in which this can be accomplished—by faith that realises the love of Christ and its effects upon us. Have we in earnest, as sinners lost and perishing, sought mercy, pardon, and peace through Him that died for us? Do we believe God's promise to grant all these things that we have prayed for? Do we humbly trust that our sins are blotted out in the blood of the Lamb, that our God is our Father, that all things are ours, and we are Christ's, and Christ is God's?

Oh, then, brethren, here is our strongest, happiest motive for faithfulness in our stewardship, in our disposal of time, money, influence, talents, of our very selves. Remember that, however difficult the task, almighty power is yours, given to all who ask it in Christ's name—the power of God the Holy Ghost. Through these motives, by this help, the yoke becomes easy, the burden light. Conscience accuses us of past unfaithfulness as stewards. Of what God has placed in our charge too much has been devoted to self, too much wasted, too much spent upon the world; little, *how little*, disposed of according to His will to Whom we and all we have belong. Yet 'if any man sin we have an Advocate with the Father, Jesus Christ the righteous: and He is the propitiation for our sins.' Laying past sin upon Him, resting all our hope on His life and death for us, on His continual intercession for us, let us with renewed earnestness redeem the time and opportunities that may yet remain to us, so that when the word goes forth from God as to each, 'Give an account of thy stewardship, for thou mayest be no longer steward,' we may be prepared most humbly, yet joyfully to render up our account. This is possible, brethren.

St. Paul was a man of like passions with ourselves, yet by the grace of God was he enabled to say, 'I am now ready to be offered, and the time of my departure is at hand. I have fought a good fight, I have finished my course, I have kept the faith: henceforth there is laid up for me a crown of righteousness, which the Lord, the righteous Judge, shall give me at that day.' (2 Tim. iv. 6-8.) To this end, Christian people, suffer me to give you one word of advice. Each morning when at prayer consider how in your day's work, your day's pleasures, your day's expenditure, how in thought, word, and deed, you can best employ for God's glory the talents committed to your charge, and ask grace and strength for the work. During each day make it your rule on certain set occasions, going out and coming in, if you will, to call to mind the truth, 'Thou God seest me.' And every evening when you kneel in prayer examine your day's life; ask yourselves how far you might have served God with the tongue, the hand, the purse, the other talents entrusted to you, and how far you *have* done so. While you ask pardon for every failure in your stewardship, remember that to-day's failures should be the best lesson for to-morrow's efforts, and so be made to contribute towards to-morrow's triumph. In the morning let your prayer be, 'Lord, what wilt Thou have me to do?' Let the solemn confession of the evening be, 'God be merciful to me a sinner.'

Finally, brethren, look onward; look beyond the day's work to the evening's repose, the rest with Christ. Beyond even that blessed rest.—look forward to the dawn, the dawning of the resurrection, the rising of the Sun of righteousness upon the endless day of eternal glory,—when all their sins, negligences, and ignorances, for ever put away, the Judge shall say to each one of those that have in faith tried to fulfil the duties of their stewardship, 'Well done, good and faithful servant: enter thou into the joy of thy Lord.'

## XIX.

### THE SAVIOUR'S REJOICING AND ITS CAUSE.

St. Luke, x., verse 21. — 'In that hour Jesus rejoiced in spirit, and said, I thank Thee, O Father, Lord of heaven and earth, that Thou hast hid these things from the wise and prudent, and hast revealed them unto babes, even so, Father, for so it seemed good in Thy sight.'

'A MAN of sorrows and acquainted with grief.' Such was the description given beforehand by Isaiah of the Redeemer promised at the Fall, who by suffering should conquer man's great enemy, and take away the sin of the world. How completely was it made in the life on earth of our Lord. I think that this is the only instance, all through the Gospels, in which we are told that the Saviour rejoiced. 'Jesus wept;' 'Jesus was grieved;' 'Jesus was troubled;' Jesus was 'in an agony;' these are the characters, for the most part, imprinted on the occurrences of His pilgrimage to the cross and grave. Self-exiled from His glorious heaven He journeyed through a world of rebels, whose sins He came to pardon, but who despised and rejected Him. He was the daily witness of a weight of sin which should add to His burden at Calvary. He was a pitiful spectator of the suffering which that sin brought upon the world of His own creation,—suffering, in which, though sinless Himself, He had come to bear His part. When you consider these things, can you wonder if we read so much of the Saviour's sorrow, and find so little of His joy? Now and then we hear a tone of exultation in His solemn words, a flash of brightness from the coming glory beams across the dark shadow of the Cross. Such lightings-up are rare, though when they do occur they illuminate the Redeemer's tender love for lost man, His sympathy with these He came to save. Tones of holy joy ring in such utterances of His as that reply to Andrew and Philip when they tell Him of the humble petition of the Gentile worshippers at the feast, 'Sir, we would see Jesus;' and Jesus answered them, saying, 'The hour is come that the Son of man should be glorified.' (St. John, xii. 21, &c.) Such joy we recognise in those most encouraging, most blessed words to the malefactor dying, saved at His side, 'To-day shalt thou be with Me in Paradise.' Such joy bursts from His expiring lips—joy for Himself, and joy for us, in that loud cry, 'It is finished.' But the language of *unal-*

*loyed* exultation can scarcely be said to have issued from His lips *on earth*. The full diapason of immortal joy first wells forth in notes that reach us from *realms of glory*, 'Fear not, I am the First and the Last; I am He that liveth, and was dead; and, behold, I am alive for evermore, Amen; and have the keys of hell and of death.' In the expression of our Saviour's joy, which I have read to you as the subject of our meditations at this time, we obtain a view not only of that part of His character which inspires us with confidence and delight, but also of that which should fill us with a holy dread and godly fear. He rejoiced in the hiding as well as in the publishing of the way of peace. So that here we behold the goodness and severity of God. Set forth in the person of the God Man Christ Jesus, we hear beforehand that terrible voice of most just judgment which shall hereafter be pronounced upon impenitent sinners (even while we listen to the words of our Saviour's joy) over them that receive the message of mercy as little children, and are saved from wrath through Him : 'I thank Thee, O Father, Lord of heaven and earth, that Thou hast hid *these things*,'—as we gather from the context, the downfall of Satan and the coming of the Kingdom of God, the way of salvation through a crucified Messiah. These were hidden by God the Father, Lord of heaven and earth, from the wise and prudent! Surely, brethren, not from the *truly* wise, the *really* prudent. Not from them of whom it is said by the Psalmist, 'Whoso is wise and will observe these things, even they shall understand the loving-kindness of the Lord.' (Ps. cvii. 41.) *Not* from those who study to be wise and observant of the ways of the Lord. *Not* from the prudent, of whom it is asserted twice by inspiration, that the 'prudent man foreseeth the evil, and hideth himself,' (Ps. xxii. 3; Ps. xxvii. 12.) *Not* from him who foresees the wrath of God in the great day, and 'hideth himself' betimes in the very heart that was riven on the cross, crying, 'Rock of Ages, rent for me, let me hide myself in Thee.' Of all these persons, says God by the prophet Hosea, 'Who is wise, and he shall understand these things? prudent, and he shall know them?' (Hos. xiv. 9.) 'That Thou hast hidden these things.' From whom? *Not* surely from such as manifest in their worldly affairs that wisdom and prudence which God has in His goodness bestowed upon them. *But* from the wise in their own conceits, from the prudent of this world, from such as despise the preaching of the cross, and look upon it as foolishness. From such as cavil at the word of God, and study it if they study it at all, only to seek for difficulties. From them that measure that word by their own fancied wisdom, and living in a little corner of the world for a few short years, would fain submit to their judgment the ways of the eternal Almighty, Lord of heaven and earth. Nor are these things hid from them *alone*, but from those also whose wisdom and prudence have brought them to the conclusion that this world is enough for them, and who devote heart and soul to earth and its concerns, and despise as dreamers those whose affections and efforts are set on things above. From them these things are hidden. and, oh, terrible truth! the Saviour rejoiced and acknowledged with thanks this hiding. It so seemed *good* in the sight of His Father, Lord of heaven and earth. Oh, most awful mystery of Divine justice, the attribute of that God Who is holy, holy, holy! Our Lord's solemn thanksgiving is present to St. Paul when speaking of himself and his brethren as preachers of the Gospel, 'We are,' he says, ' unto God a sweet savour of Christ in them that are saved, and in them that perish.' (2 Cor. i. 15.) My brethren, are there among us any to whom godliness appears to be an unwise sacrificing of this world to another?—any who doubt the truth of the word of God?—any to whom the way of salvation set forth therein appears too simple?—any who despise it and to whom when preached it is foolishness? Beware lest you be in reality among the people here spoken of. In what spirit have you approached the subject of religion? Have you considered it in reliance on your own wisdom and prudence as alone sufficient to understand and to judge of that which may be set before you? Have you determined to believe only that which may in your opinion appear probable or even possible? Have you resolved to embrace no religious system but that which suits *your* ideas and fitness? Do you read the Bible that you may find out whether you approve it or no? Do you come to this great subject as to one which it would be neither wise nor prudent to put in the place of paramount importance, and of all-absorbing interest? If so, I pray you remember that the Father, Lord of heaven and earth, hath seen good to hide the truths of salvation from those who, like you, are wise and prudent in their own conceits, that through this hiding it is that the preaching of the cross is foolishness to you; that those to whom that preaching is foolishness are those that *perish*. And that this terrible hiding of the truth from you is so right, so just, so necessary to the great scheme of God's providence, that in His rare rejoicing the Saviour rejoiced in this, and on this account made thankful acknowledgment to God. Oh, brethren, if you would escape the infliction of so ruinous a blindness, learn from our text what disposition is required from those to whom God will reveal the things that concern their everlasting peace, 'I thank Thee that Thou hast hid these things from the wise and prudent, and hast revealed them unto babes;' unto such as, whether by nature, wise and prudent, or the reverse, are simply desirous to learn the will of God when they have learned to obey. They bring no theories, no prejudices of their own to God, but come before Him with the cry, 'Lord, what wilt Thou have me to do?' They come as little children to their Father, stretching forth the hand that He may hold and guide them safely home. Thus they approach the revealed word of God, using such wisdom and prudence as He has given them to learn whether it be His word, but committing themselves in prayer to Him for guidance in so solemn a matter; then when led to see that it comes indeed from Him who liveth and abideth for ever, bending in lowliness to take it at His hands, 'It is written,' suffices them as it sufficed their Lord; they ask no more. In this humble spirit himself Saul of Tarsus the learned, Apollos the eloquent, and Cornelius the noble, came to know the way of salvation; came as simply and as trustingly as the woman of Bethany or the fishermen of Galilee. From them God hid nothing that they needed to know. To them He revealed the things that were hidden from prudent

Pharisees and learned scribes. These had the word of God in their hands, and professed to understand it: but indirect as the whole book is with the testimony of Jesus, they found no Saviour there. On the other hand, see that Ethiopian trying humbly to learn the will of God, poring over the prophecy of Isaiah, as he makes that long return journey from the house of God at Jerusalem. Rather than such an one shall perish in ignorance, a teacher is sent him by an angel, being caught away again by the Spirit of the Lord directly his work is done, but not until to the man or childlike spirit these things, even Jesus and His salvation, have been revealed, not before the fountain in the desert has witnessed to his faith in Christ, and the happy Christian has gone on his way rejoicing in a Saviour.

I believe that much of the scepticism of these days arises from the fact that men approach religion rather from an intellectual than from an emotional point of view. They measure it by the intellect instead of receiving it with the heart. Now what is the disposition of the little child as referred to in my text? Is it not one of simple, obedient love? If so, what disposition can be so suited for receiving His Gospel, who, though His wisdom be infinite, never says of Himself, 'God is wisdom,' though He be almighty, never says, 'God is power.' Yet does He say of Himself, 'God is love.' Men, wise and prudent men of this world are seeking to fathom the mystery of existence. A mystery hidden in the 'I Am,' the self-existent Jehovah. They have failed, and *will* fail. He was a wise man who said of old, 'Canst thou by searching find out God?' (Job, xv. 7.) But where the philosopher fails the babe succeeds. Humble, trusting hearts do seek and find their God, loving faith discovers her Lord in the crucified of Calvary, and follows Him to the right hand of the Father, and rests beneath His arm, almighty to save. My brethren, this childlike disposition towards God is not of human origin. It is not natural, either to the wise or the ignorant, of unconverted men. It is the gift of God. Withheld from none that seek it aright; you that have it not pray that it may be given you, lest being without it the way of life be for ever hidden from your eyes. And if any of you trust that this spirit has been granted you by the Holy Ghost, cultivate and cherish a gift so valuable, so necessary, all along your journey of life. Walking with God in that spirit, He will show you by the way all that it is well for you to know, and will bring you safely to your journey's end, ·For,' saith Christ, 'it is not the will of your Father which is in heaven that one of these little ones should perish.'

## XX.

### THE WORK OF THE CHURCH, AND OF EACH MEMBER THEREOF.

St. Matthew, x., part of verse 7.—'As ye go, preach.'

AT the outset of our Lord's public ministry, great multitudes were drawn together by His works of mercy and by the voice of His teaching. He came with power in word and work unknown before. The authority and spirituality of His preaching was not only a new thing to His hearers, but it reached their hearts, it appealed to their consciences, and men felt that there was in it that which supplied the need of their souls. And so they pressed upon Him, they were very attentive to hear Him.

Saving the preparatory ministrations of John the Baptist, there was at that time a very famine of this kind of instruction. The authorised teachers of the Word were unfaithful to their trust—gave stones instead of bread, filling men's minds with foolish traditions and ritual observances, rather than the lessons of history, and the prophetic promises to be found in the Old Testament, which they professed to revere. The people had no faithful shepherds. The seekers for God were a scattered flock; and awakened souls fainted for want of some to guide them into the way of peace. So the loving Lord pitied them, and bid His disciples pray for them (ch. ix. 36–38): 'But when He saw the multitudes, He was moved with compassion on them, because they fainted, and were scattered abroad, as sheep having no shepherd. Then saith He unto His disciples, The harvest truly is plenteous, but the labourers are few. Pray ye therefore the Lord of the harvest, that He will send forth labourers into His harvest.' And our Lord gave effect to His compassion by sending forth His disciples with this commission (ch. x. 6–8), 'But go rather to the lost sheep of the house of Israel. And as ye go, preach, saying, The kingdom of heaven is at hand. Heal the sick, cleanse the lepers, raise the dead, cast out devils: freely ye have received, freely give.' Such was the first commission given to the Church of Christ; such the first intimation of that which was to become the life-work of that Church, and of every member thereof.

We take as our text its leading words, 'As ye go, preach.' Go and do every work of mercy, and kindness, and love, that comes within your power and opportunity. Go and do good freely, as God hath done to you. 'And as ye go, preach.' Few and brief but glorious words, brethren, to be afterwards defined, enlarged, and confirmed by the life and doctrine of the Lord and His *inspired* servants. The work was at first limited in its extent (ch. x. 5. 6); 'These twelve Jesus sent forth, and commanded them, saying, Go not into the way of the Gentiles, and into any city of the Samaritans enter ye not: but go rather to the lost sheep of the house of Israel;' but it was afterwards to become universal (ch. xxviii. 19); 'Go ye therefore, and teach all nations, baptizing them in the name of the Father, and of the Son, and of the Holy Ghost.' The proclamation of an approaching salvation was to be exchanged for the preaching of a *finished* redemption (verse 7), 'Go quickly and tell His disciples that He is risen from the dead; and, behold, He goeth before you into Galilee; there shall ye see Him.' And it became the preaching of Him, 'Who hath delivered us from the power of darkness, and hath translated us into the kingdom of His dear Son; in Whom we have redemption through His blood, even the forgiveness of sins.'

The commission given to the twelve, and specially given to the ministry of the Church, as to men whose *whole* attention was to be devoted to its fulfilment, was yet to embrace in its requirements the entire body of the Church. To every spiritual member of it, says St. Peter in his first Epistle, ii. 9–12, ' But ye are a chosen generation, a royal priesthood, an holy nation, a peculiar people ; that ye should show forth the praises of Him Who hath called you out of darkness into His marvellous light : which in time past were not a people, but are now the people of God ; which had not obtained mercy, but now have obtained mercy. Dearly beloved, I beseech you as strangers and pilgrims, abstain from fleshly lusts which war against the soul ; having your conversation honest among the Gentiles ; that, whereas they speak against you as evildoers, they may by your good works, which they shall behold, glorify God in the day of visitation.' Yet, further, notice concerning this commission, that the teaching by it commanded was to be aided and confirmed by the power of a holy life. St. Peter inculcates this in the verses I have just read to you ; and our Lord commands the same in St. Matt. v. 16 : ' Let your light so shine before men, that they may see your good works, and glorify your Father which is in heaven.' And observe, also, that the preaching here described is not to be a mere proclaiming of love and goodwill, whether on the part of God to man, or of man to God and to His fellows. The kingdom of heaven *then* to be proclaimed as *at hand*, and *afterwards* as *opened* to all believers, is represented in the Scriptures not as a mere dream of universal love and peace, but as a definite system of faith, duty, and reward; as a way, a narrow way, leading to life; a name, an only name, given under heaven among men, whereby we may be saved; a gospel, than which if an angel from heaven preach any other, we are to hold him accursed.

The preaching of the Church is to be dogmatic, but the dogmatics are not to be of men, but of God. This limitation of preaching is strictly enforced by St. Paul (Titus, i. 7, 9): 'A bishop (says he) must be blameless, as the steward of God. . . . Holding fast the faithful word as he hath been taught, that he may be able by sound doctrine both to exhort and to convince the gainsayers.' And Titus himself is charged (Titus, ii. 11 to end): 'For the grace of God that bringeth salvation hath appeared to all men, teaching us that, denying ungodliness and worldly lusts, we should live soberly, righteously, and godly, in this present world; looking for that blessed hope, and the glorious appearing of the great God and our Saviour Jesus Christ; Who gave Himself for us, that He might redeem us from all iniquity, and purify unto Himself a peculiar people, zealous of good works. These things speak, and exhort, and rebuke with all authority. Let no man despise thee.'

Such, dear brethren, is the commission given to the Church of Christ, and to each faithful member thereof. Go on your way rejoicing in God your Saviour; go as men who have found Christ to be indeed wisdom, righteousness, sanctification, and redemption; go as men who are not their own, but bought with a price; go as men hasting from time to eternity; go, doing your duty in the world and to the world, but ' as ye go, preach!' Preach Christ as ' the Way, the Truth, and the Life.'

Now see, brethren, how this great commission was obeyed by those to whom it was given, and such as soon afterwards were joined to them. We read of them in various circumstances, in scattered places, and among widely differing classes and nations. But, wherever they were, before whomsoever they came, in every stage of the great journey of life, ' as they went, they preached.' And the subject of their preaching was *Jesus* crucified and risen,—as the way, the only way, by which lost man might find God, by which ruined man might be restored, by which sinful man might obtain holiness, and dying man enter into life eternal. Honoured or despised, received or persecuted, at home or abroad, they went about doing good, and as they went, they *preached*. When public attention was first called to them after the ascension, they preached (Acts. ii. 23, 24, 38); 'Him, being delivered by the determinate counsel and foreknowledge of God, ye have taken, and by wicked hands have crucified and slain: Whom God hath raised up, having loosed the pains of death: because it was not possible that He should be holden of it. . . . Then Peter said unto them, Repent, and be baptized every one of you in the name of Jesus Christ for the remission of sins, and ye shall receive the gift of the Holy Ghost.' Having wrought a great miracle to the astonishment of the beholders they *preached* (Acts, iii. 15, 16); 'And ye killed the Prince of life, Whom God hath raised from the dead, whereof ye are witnesses. And His name through faith in His name hath made this man strong, whom ye see and know: yea, the faith which is by Him hath given him this perfect soundness in the presence of you all.' Brought before rulers, they *preached* (Acts, v. 30, 31); 'The God of our fathers raised up Jesus, Whom ye slew, and hanged on a tree. Him hath God exalted with His right hand to be a Prince and a Saviour, for to give repentance to Israel, and forgiveness of sins.' In the prison at Philippi they *preached* (Acts, xvi.

30, 31); 'And he brought them out and said, Sirs, what must I do to be saved? And they said, Believe on the Lord Jesus Christ, and thou shalt be saved, and thy house.' So at learned Athens (Acts, xvii. 31, 32); 'He hath appointed a day in the which He will judge the world in righteousness by that Man whom He hath ordained: whereof He hath given assurance unto all men, in that He hath raised Him from the dead. And when they heard of the resurrection of the dead, some mocked; and others said, We will hear thee again of this matter.' And before governors and kings (Acts, xxvi. 22, 23); 'Having therefore obtained help of God, I continue unto this day, witnessing both to small and great, saying none other things than those which the prophets and Moses did say should come: that Christ should suffer, and that He should be the first that should rise from the dead, and should show light unto the people, and to the Gentiles.' And at imperial and warlike Rome (Acts, xxviii. 30, 31); 'And Paul dwelt two whole years in his own hired house, and received all that came in unto him, preaching the kingdom of God, and teaching those things which concern the Lord Jesus Christ with all confidence, no man forbidding him.' But here it may be said, you have been giving us instances of the preaching of which you have spoken, but the preachers you have mentioned were all of them Apostles, preachers of the word by calling and profession. Can you show that it was the duty and the habit of private Christians also to set forth the way of life to their fellow-sinners?

My brethren, we must not forget that we have not in the New Testament any formal record of the acts of private Christians. We must, therefore, gather what information we can about them from the incidental mention made of them, here and there, in the history and writings of members of the 'glorious company.' Now, we find that a great dispersion of the Christians of Jerusalem took place after the death of St. Stephen, the proto-martyr, and we are told (Acts, viii. 4); 'Therefore they that were scattered abroad went everywhere *preaching the Word.*' There were in the Church in those days two excellent persons, a husband and a wife, working tent-makers, by name Aquila and Priscilla. These meeting with a fervent and devout man, Apollos, who knew not the Gospel, 'took him unto them, and expounded unto him the way of God more perfectly.' (Acts, xviii. 26.) Luke, a physician among *men;* among *women,* Tryphena and Tryphosa, and Persis, are spoken of as fellow-workers with St. Paul, and as labouring much in the Lord. Phœbe is commended as a servant or deaconess of the Church; Urbane, as a helper in Christ.

Indeed, brethren, from all we read, both in Holy Scripture and in the works of Christian historians, we see that of the early Christians, male or female, ministers and people, it was true, most emphatically true, that 'as they went, they *preached.*' None intruding themselves uncalled, unordained, into the offices of the ministry, yet one and all considering it their sacred duty to help, by word, by example, by assistance, and encouragement, in the great life-work of the Church, the bringing in of all, so far as they could *reach*, to believe in Him Who loved them, and gave Himself for them. And, surely, brethren, if we have indeed received the truth to the saving of our souls, if Christ is to us 'Jehovah our righteousness,' if we desire to be made like to Him Whom we hope perfectly to resemble when we see Him as He is, surely we shall not rest satisfied unless we are bearing our share in the work that brought Him from heaven to earth, from the throne to His Cross, His grave, His resurrection. As He went on His way, 'a man of sorrows,' to make many glad for ever; on His way to suffer, and by suffering to save; as He went, He preached repentance, faith and holiness,—Himself as the one Saviour, —Himself as the one image of God the Father;

and the Holy Spirit, and all His promised gifts of grace. *These* were the subjects of His preaching. He preached by His words, in the temple, and by the way, in the synagogues, and in the cornfields : to the scribes and Pharisees, to the multitudes and the poor, to the publicans and harlots : in the fishing-boat on the lake and resting on the well, to the Samaritan woman and her friends. Living, He preached as He went, by His life and example; dying, He preached by His holy, blessed death. His last convert was made upon the Cross ; the thief, whom expiring He won, and took home to be with Him in Paradise.

My brethren of the laity, when I call on you to take part in this holy work, I do not exhort you, (God forbid!) to assume uncalled, unauthorised, unordained, the offices of the ministry of the Church. It is ordered by God, and in the nature of the work it is necessary, that men should be commissioned and set apart, whose whole time and study and powers should be devoted to the guidance and government, the instruction and edification, of the Church ; and who, by that very devotion, are unfitted for the performance of those secular duties, and filling of those secular offices which are, in God's providence, to be performed and filled by the laity. Yet, there is work for God which all may do, and are bound to do, and for *some* share in which no Christian can say that he is wholly unfit. When the ordained ministers of Christ have done their best, (and God forgive our feeble efforts, our scanty labours, for His Son's sake!) yet, how much remains to be done, that we cannot do, how many remain uninvited whom we cannot reach. In the training up in our most holy faith of such as in baptism we have offered to Christ, in the instruction of the younger members of your households, Christian parents, Christian employers, Christian masters, and mistresses, how many opportunities you have of preaching Christ which are denied to us. Look at the young men of our shops, factories, and fields, how few come to church! At work all day, weary at night, they are well-nigh out of our reach. Who is to call them? Surely each young Christian workman, each Christian neighbour, should have a loving voice to warn and to invite them. By the sick bed, each Christian nurse; among neighbours, each believing neighbour, should tell of our Redeemer. If each Church-going man or woman would try to bring one more, how full our churches would soon be! Preach Christ thus, preach Christ one and all. Let the rich Christian not be ashamed to own Christ at his dinner-table, to take the Christian side, to rebuke ungodly conversation, by a grieving, sorrowful silence. Let the poor man own Christ, in the midst of swearing, or infidel fellow-workmen. Let the Christian servant own Christ in a kitchen full of sneering fellow-servants.

Brethren, there is work for all, opportunity for all. The Holy Ghost is promised to give strength to all, (oh, pray for Him!) a crown for all, who will preach Christ. Yes, brethren, 'as ye go, preach.' At every opportunity, as you travel on to your account, preach. Seek grace by your consistent life and holy, peaceful death, to proclaim the one Saviour. No human praise may follow your efforts, no prize of eloquence reward your words. Yet, it is no slight honour to be called to work with God, no mean dignity to be invited to walk in a way hallowed by the footprints of Him, Who 'went about doing good.' Each pleading word you speak for Christ is noted and approved by Him, and will be recalled by Him when 'They that be wise shall shine as the brightness of the firmament ; and they that turn many to righteousness, as the stars, for ever and ever.' (Dan. xii. 3.)

## XXI.

### THE DWELLING-PLACE OF THE LORD.

1 KINGS, viii. 27.—'Will God indeed dwell on the earth? Behold, the heaven and heaven of heavens cannot contain Thee; how much less this house that I have builded?'

A WEIGHTY question! for the presence of God is necessary to create and to sustain any spiritual life in our hearts, and since in our sinful and mortal state we cannot even find Him, far less reach Him, it is necessary that God should come to us, that He should indeed dwell on the earth; else we shall never be enabled to dwell in heaven.

'Will God indeed dwell on the earth?' inquires King Solomon. Then, as if in answer to his own question, he adds, 'Behold, the heaven and heaven of heavens cannot contain Thee; how much less this house that I have builded?' Why so? Because God is *infinite*. The meaning of that word is beyond the power of men or angels to conceive. The only idea that we can gain of infinity is by comparison. For instance, let us compare the vast expanse of the sky with the little spot of earth on which we stand; or the lapse of ages with a moment of time. Let us work out the thought here suggested to us by Solomon, and lift up our eyes to the heavens above, and let us try to realise the millions of miles that lie between us and the nearest of those fixed stars that nightly shine upon the earth. Could we pass over that distance by a miracle, in a moment, we should find that God was there. Could we go on thus travelling and pass over the like distance each moment of eternity, God would yet be before and behind and around us; we should be as far as ever from escaping His presence, the gaze of His all-seeing eye, or the power of His almighty hand. 'Whither,' says David, 'shall I flee from Thy Spirit? or whither shall I flee from Thy presence? If I ascend up into heaven, Thou art there; if I make my bed in hell (Hades), behold, Thou art there. If I take the wings of the morning, and dwell in the uttermost parts of the sea, even there shall Thy hand lead me, and Thy right hand shall hold me.' (Ps. cxxxix. 7–10.) What a striking commentary we have here upon the language of our text! Will such a God as this dwell on the earth?

My brethren, there is among men of every

age and country a universal persuasion that, in some way or other, God *does* dwell on earth, and manifest His presence in certain places in a special manner. The temples, some so magnificent, some so lowly; the images and symbols, so varied, so countless, of the heathen, are all prepared in the belief that God inhabits them, and with a vague idea that it is good for man that He should so dwell on earth. It may be remarked upon this subject that if God is everywhere present, of course He is present on earth also. But this general presence is not that to which Solomon refers, nor is it that looked for by the builders of the heathen temples or makers of the heathen idols. They for the most part believed that their gods were actually contained in the idols which, and in the places where, they worshipped. Solomon knew and confessed this to be impossible. But with regard to an especial manifestation of God's presence with man, and some plain token of His dwelling here below, we must look to Holy Scripture for a reply to his question. The Bible gives us an affirmative answer, and tells us that God has indeed thus dwelt on the earth.

To Adam before the fall God spake as a man speaketh unto his friend; and after the fall the Lord walked in Eden, and while He gave sentence on our guilty parents, gave also the promise of a Saviour, who should deprive that sentence of its bitterness, and rob death of its sting. God conversed with Noah, and appeared often to Abraham. God yielded to the prayerful wrestling of Jacob. He revealed Himself to Moses as the 'I Am' at the burning bush in Horeb. God was in the pillar of His glory, whence looking forth, He troubled the Egyptian host. He showed Himself to the elders of Israel on Sinai, and passed by Moses when hidden in the cleft of the rock, the sign of Christ.

In answer to this prayer of Solomon, God's glory filled the Temple, so that the priests could not enter because the glory of the Lord had filled the Lord's house. By that same bright appearance, the Shechinah, God dwelt between the cherubim upon the mercy-seat over the ark. God was in the still small voice that spake to Elijah in the wilderness, and walked in the furnace with Shadrach, Meshach, and Abednego. And when the fulness of the appointed time was come, God took our nature upon Him, and was made in the likeness of man. Then He did indeed dwell on the earth, to bear earth's iniquity and restore lost man to God. He did not abhor the Virgin's womb, He did not despise the manger, He dwelt in poverty, reproach, and contempt; He dwelt on the cross, He dwelt in the grave, and though now He is at the right hand of God He dwells on the earth still. 'I will not leave you comfortless; I will come to you,' He said to His sorrowing disciples. By the spiritual presence of the Father and of the Son—by the coming of the Holy Ghost—the Holy Trinity, three Persons in one God, God still dwells on earth,—He dwells with His spiritual Church and in the heart of each believer. Sacraments and ordinances, prayers and praises, sermons and exhortations, can receive life and reality from the presence of God the Holy Ghost, and from that alone. Christ offers Himself to dwell with each one who will open unto Him : 'Behold, I stand at the door, and knock : if any man hear My voice, and open the door, I will come in to him, and will sup with him, and he with Me.' And the presence of God the Father is thus promised by our Lord in St. John, xiv. 23 : 'If a man love Me, he will keep My words : and My Father will love him, and We will come unto him, and make Our abode with him.'

How, then, may we obtain the benefit of so blessed an offer ? How may a man so open his heart to the entrance of his Lord and his God as to bring Him in there for ever to abide? Grace must first cast out from our hearts all that would take Christ's place in them. All self-righteousness and dependence on anything of our own for salvation must be put away. *For salvation* we must look to Him alone, who has wrought out an everlasting salvation for us; to Him who only can be to us our wisdom, righteousness, sanctification, and redemption, our all, in God the Father's sight. Every idol must be dethroned, if He is to dwell in us; He must reign supreme. Friends, pleasures, health, strength, life itself, all must give way before *Him*. These things we may lawfully care for, but we must love, esteem, and value Him infinitely above them all. Sin must be striven against and overcome; sinful habits and lusts mortified, and the flesh crucified with all its vile affections.

Moreover, there is a certain peculiar temper and disposition of mind required in them with whom God will stoop to dwell: ' For thus saith the high and lofty One that inhabiteth eternity, whose name is Holy; I dwell in the high and holy place, with him also that is of a contrite and humble spirit, to revive the spirit of the humble, and to revive the heart of the contrite ones.' (Isa. lvii. 15.) Contrition and humility are requisite where the Lord God is to come in and dwell,—the deepest sense of guilt, the deepest sorrow for sin, grief and shame on account of it. When we confess ourselves 'miserable sinners,' we too often scarcely enter into the spirit of those words. 'I abhor myself,' said Job. Could we, as he did, see more clearly something of the unspeakable holiness of God; could we see ourselves as He sees us from Whom no secrets are hid; could we feel more of His love of holiness and hatred of iniquity, then indeed should we be truly humble in spirit, and attain to that broken and contrite heart in which He will not disdain to dwell. Then should we enjoy the blessed experience promised by Christ, 'At that day ye shall know that I am in My Father, and ye in Me, and I in you.' But here again occurs the question, How can we so fit and prepare ourselves to be the dwelling of our God? Can we make clean our hearts within us? and can those hearts of themselves become broken and contrite?

Brethren, herein consists the wonderful suitability of the Gospel to our case—that everything necessary to salvation which we have *not*, everything that is to be done in us as well as for us, is provided for therein. God the Holy Ghost will work this great change that is required to prepare us to be the dwelling-place of the Lord. He will create in us clean hearts and renew right spirits within us. He will give us such a sight of our sin as will lead us to Christ crucified for mercy. *He* will take from us all depend-

p 2

ence on any righteousness or repentance of our own: *He* will give us faith to believe in the Lord Jesus, living, dying, risen, and interceding for us; and, at the sight of a holy Saviour agonized for our sin, He will melt our hard hearts into penitence, and make us to mourn for and hate the sin that once we loved. This is the promise of God: ' Then will I sprinkle clean water upon you, and ye shall be clean: from all your filthiness, and from all your idols, will I cleanse you. A new heart also will I give you, and a new spirit will I put within you: and I will take away the stony heart out of your flesh, and I will give you an heart of flesh. And I will put my Spirit within you, and cause you to walk in my statutes, and ye shall keep my judgments, and do them.' (Ezek. xxxvi. 25–27.)

Let us call on God to fulfil this His gracious word, to begin or to carry on this work in us. We may claim it of Him for Jesus' sake, and our claim will be allowed and granted. Let us claim it as an inestimable blessing. If God, Whom the heaven of heavens cannot contain, dwell on earth, *dwell in us*, what can we want that is really good? whom need we fear but Him? In prosperity He will keep us holy and humble; in adversity He will be our comfort and our stay; in life our support, in death our life, and in eternity our triumph and our exceeding great reward. Remember that, except we have this Divine presence in us, we are *lost*. 'Know ye not your own selves' (says St. Paul) 'how that Jesus Christ is in you, except ye be reprobates?' (2 Cor. xiii. 5.) *Reprobates*—rejected of God, and under sentence of death eternal. What need have we to pray—

> 'Abide with me from morn till eve,
> For without Thee I cannot live;
> Abide with me when night is nigh,
> For without Thee I dare not die.'

'Will God indeed dwell on the earth?' says Solomon: 'behold, the heaven and heaven of heavens cannot contain Thee; how much less this house that I have builded?' The Most High dwelleth not in temples made with hands; neither the lofty spire, nor the long aisle, nor the beautiful windows, nor the pealing organ, can bring Him down on earth. These things may help to solemnise our minds, and to inspire emotion, but they are as nothing in His sight. Yet He will dwell in the houses that we raise to the honour of His name. They cannot *contain* Him, indeed, but when filled with worshippers of contrite and believing spirit, the Most High is there among them; where even two or three are gathered together in His name, He has promised to be in the midst of them.

My brethren, do you show your value for His presence by your regular attendance and devout behaviour in the house where prayer is wont to be made? Be mindful of the purpose for which you come there—for prayer and praise, and to be nurtured in Gospel truth and ordinances. Do not, even in appearance, leave the work of praise and prayer to the clergy and official persons. When you lift up your *hearts*, lift up your *voices*, too. There is no sound so beautiful as the sound of many voices with one accord calling upon and extolling their God, and saying Amen at the giving of thanks.

So is the house of prayer on earth a portal to the home of praise above, where St. John, in prophetic vision, 'heard a voice as the voice of many waters, and as the voice of a great thunder, the voice of harpers harping with their harps, and the voice of them that sung as it were a new song before the throne'—that song no man could learn 'but they which were redeemed from the earth.'

## XXII.

### THE POSITION OF A TRUE CHRISTIAN, AS ILLUSTRATED BY THE POSITION OF THE HEALED DEMONIAC.

St. Luke, viii., part of verse 35.—'Sitting at the feet of Jesus, clothed, and in his right mind.'

A FEW hours before he was wandering in the mountains and in the tombs that, after the fashion of that country, were hewn out in their rocky sides. For a long time this had been his most miserable case. He had no peace. Day and night were alike to him. Chains and fetters were insufficient to restrain him. Tearing them asunder and breaking them in pieces he fled from his keepers and roamed in desert places crying and cutting himself with stones. From St. Matt. viii. 28, we learn that, with a companion in the same wretched condition, he had made the neighbourhood of their haunts unsafe for travellers: they were 'exceeding fierce, so that no man might pass by that way;' their bodies the habitation of a legion of evil spirits; they seemed to be given up to Satan as his helpless, hopeless prey. Now we have one of them at least, sitting at the feet of Jesus, clothed, and in his right mind. Christ hath spoken the word, and Satan with his armies hath fled discomfited. Look at the once fierce and dangerous demoniac; the savage fire has gone from his eyes, his naked, bleeding limbs are covered and clothed; his wild, weary wanderings are ended; he is happy, looking up to his Lord. He cannot bear to leave Him, and is beseeching Him that he may continue with Him. I will not at this time, brethren, speak to you on the general subject of the miracle. I wish, as I think I may lawfully do, to take the words of our text, and use them as descriptive of the condition of the man whom redeeming love and grace have delivered from the power of Satan; of him who, having been brought to repentance and faith in Christ, is justified, and has peace with God through Him. I would speak of men as they ought to be, and as they might be: striving to fulfil the vows of their baptism, and to live in the enjoyment of the privileges secured to them by the Christian Covenant. Take the words in order, and you have the Christian described,—

(I.) First as at rest, 'sitting at the feet of Jesus.' Whatever may be the pleasures and profits of that state, which I must call worldliness, I mean the state of him who is not living the life which he now lives in the flesh, by the faith of the Son of God,—tranquil restfulness of mind is not one of them. The unconverted man is ever reaching forward to something or other, which is, he thinks, to satisfy his best desires, to afford him true contentment, to lead him to repose. His search, his efforts, are alike, vain. Each object of desire is cast aside almost as soon as it is attained, and then, man turns his attention to, and sets his heart upon another; for each object, as he grasps it, fails to satisfy: he finds that he wants something further; in none of them can he find repose. Rank and honour, wisdom and learning, wealth and leisure, luxuries and pleasure, let him attain them all, yet all are not enough. He is not satisfied, he thirsts for something else; he has not found rest to his soul. And as his day draws to its close, and his sun verges towards the west, and the shadows of night fall thick and fast around him, how often is he to be found wandering among the sepulchres of joys departed. While he possessed them they did not satisfy him, yet bitterly he laments them now that he knows they will return to him no more. As to his eternal prospects, he turns away his eyes as far as he can from them, for he has no certain hope, no well-grounded assurance of his safety. Some vague, baseless hopes he may entertain; some general idea that he will be no worse off than many of his neighbours, but that is all. He dares not think much or deeply on the subject; or, if he does, it is in the vain effort to shake off all belief in the justice of God, or even in the existence of the Most High, for on these subjects (the most deeply interesting that can engage the attention of a reasoning creature) he has no rest. On the other hand, where Christ has cast down Satan from his usurped lordship over the soul—where He has spoken the word of power, 'Come unto Me;' then he has kept the word of promise, 'I will give you rest.' He has delivered His servant from that uneasy fear of coming wrath which allows a man to have no settled peace. He has removed the burden of guilt away from him, and enabled him to take to himself the full, free redemption of the cross. He enables him to apply to the salvation of his own soul those triumphant words of His: 'It is finished.' He enables him so to believe this as to rest upon it, and in it. Being justified by faith the believer has peace with God through our Lord Jesus Christ; that peace brings with it the Spirit of Adoption, and the Spirit of Adoption involves in itself the hope of glory. He that is reconciled to God is made a child of God; and if a child then an heir, an heir of God, and a joint-heir with Christ. Having this hope, and in proportion as he cherishes and cultivates it, the Christian man is delivered from those restless cares and anxieties that so torment the unconverted. Earthly things may, and do too often, disturb him, but they can no longer overthrow the rest of his soul. His heart is surely fixed there where true joys are to be found. His affections are set on things above, *not* on things on the earth, for his treasure is in heaven, and 'where the treasure is, there the heart is also.' He is at rest, sitting at the feet of Jesus. Looking up to Him, the God-man, he perceives the safety of that which he has entrusted to Him. Looking up to that Divine countenance, so glorious in infinite power and might, so bright with unspeakable love; contemplating the victory that He hath won for him; considering the eternity of *His* existence, and with it the unchangeableness of *His* counsel, he sits at His feet, and is at rest: 'No foe can rob him of his Lord,' nothing can separate him from the love of Christ.

It is remarkable in reading the Acts and Epistles of the Apostles of the Lord, to see how this resting spirit had filled their souls. As to health or sickness, need or abundance, prison or freedom; nay, as to life or death—salvation, eternity. You see in them no restlessness, no uneasiness, no unsatisfied longing; only those desires which are in themselves a sweet satisfaction in life and death—to glorify God, and to enjoy more of His presence and His love.

(II.) Secondly, this man thus resting at his Saviour's feet, awhile since a naked, loathsome savage, was clothed and covered. Brethren, the condition of a believer in Christ is in this respect contrasted with the natural state of man. The natural man says to God, 'I was afraid because I was naked, and I hid myself.' The Christian dares to sit at the very feet of Jesus because he is clothed. The natural man hath nought wherewith he may hide his sin and his shame; no deeds, no gifts, of his can cover him. All that he can do, all that he can offer, is polluted by his leprous touch. He stands, trembling and speechless, in the presence of Him that hates sin, against whom he hath sinned, and who shall come to be his judge. Oh, wonder of grace! beholding the man's uncleanness with horror unspeakable, God the Son pours forth His own blood, and bids the man wash therein, and cleanse his sin away. God the Son brings forth the best robe of His own righteousness, and Himself clothes the man therewith. He is justified; where are his sins? That blood is powerful to cleanse a whole eternity—a universe of sin: where his utter want of righteousness? That righteousness could clothe a world of transgressors. So washed, so arrayed, the man hides himself no more. He is not afraid, but sits happy and contented at his Saviour's feet. He looks up into that pure and most holy face, and by contemplation is led to conformity; he studies the pattern, and the Holy Spirit enables him to copy it. Sitting at the feet of Jesus is no fruitless indolence of soul and life. It is such a learning of Him as leads the believer to put on Christ; to be clothed with His *likeness*, as well as with His merits, and so to grow in grace, and to be changed from glory to glory, even as by the Spirit of the Lord.

(III.) Once again we have this man at the feet of Jesus described as *in his right mind*. The expression, if we examine into it, is singularly apt as a description of the condition of a true Christian. This man, now in his right mind, was a few hours ago the sport, the victim of the worst passions, played upon by Satan as his instrument. What else is the natural man in general? True, he is controlled by a regard for his own reputation, by the dread of human law and human vengeance, by the love of those naturally dear to him. These and other such considerations restrain him often from the outward indulgence of his carnal appetites, yet do they rage and burn within him. Could you look into his soul as

God does, you would see it as a cage of unclean birds; and at times they overcome all the restraints of prudent selfishness and hurry their slave to destruction of body and spirit. They do, as it were, open the doors to Satan, and give place to the devil, and deliver the man, bound into his power, carried hither and thither by the surging of vile lusts; the miserable creature has no repose of soul. To heal one whose inner man is thus diseased, power must be given him, not only to restrain the outward manifestations of corrupt affections, but to stay their inward growth, and to crucify and put them to death, continually mortifying them, and daily proceeding in all virtue and godliness of living. He must be brought to 'his right mind.' The original Greek word signifies having the command of his passions, being able to direct and control them. When Christ speaks to the soul He gives this power, this command. He not only causes the unclean spirit to come out of the man, but He sends from the Father the Holy Spirit to enter into the man, and to make his body His Temple, to create in him a clean heart, and to renew in him a right spirit. That Holy Ghost is Almighty to sanctify as Christ is Almighty to redeem. However strong the lusts and passions of fallen nature, His grace is sufficient to subdue them, enabling the Christian daily and hourly to contend with, and finally to overcome them. In his strength the believer strives ever more and more successfully to be pure in heart, as well as moral in life. In the sight of God he is 'in his right mind,' at the feet of Jesus. This gift, as well as every other good gift, is to be had there, and enjoyed there, and there alone. Rest of soul, the white robe of righteousness, the gift of a right mind, through the work of the Holy Ghost, all are to be received from the Father through the Lord Jesus Christ alone. May you and I, brethren, be found there sitting and clothed, and in our right mind! What temptations, what sins, what passions, can keep from his feet the soul that hears His voice when He says, 'Come unto Me!'

## XXIII.

### PRAYING ALWAYS WITH ALL PRAYER AND SUPPLICATION IN THE SPIRIT.

Eph. vi. 18, first part.—' Praying always with all prayer and supplication in the Spirit.'

SO clear, so numerous are the invitations to prayer, and even the commands to pray, that he who believes not in the efficacy of prayer has forsaken Christian doctrine ; whilst he who lives not in the practice of prayer has abandoned the rule of Christian life. Prayer, in the full meaning of the word, is far more than asking for such things as we desire. Prayer is the voice of the soul to the soul's Creator—the going forth of the spirit of man to the Father of spirits. It is a necessity of human nature, generally felt. Travel through the world and you will not find a tribe so barbarous as to be without some desire to hold converse with the powers of the unseen world—some idea of a Great Spirit or spirits to be addressed, to whom prayer is acceptable. Prayer is the soul of man conscious, even in the midst of death, and dying of immortality, and seeking to attain to it; in the midst of weakness conscious of a power, and seeking that power for a friend. The soul floating on the ocean of eternity and searching out a firm anchorage—a Rock which it may grapple, to be tossed no more. Prayer therefore, at the outset, involves faith, inasmuch as its object is invisible. Even the heathen who bows before a stock or a stone does so usually only because he believes it to be the representative of One whom he cannot see, but in whom he believes. So saith the Scripture : ' He that cometh to God must believe that *He is*.' (Heb. xi. 6.) The very act of prayer is an expression of the first words of the Creed, ' I believe in God.' Prayer has in it the conviction that the voice of the soul can reach the Being to Whom it is addressed, that it has power to influence Him—to touch His heart : that in some way or other He will take notice of it and answer it ; that His nature is such that the answer will be good for us and not evil ;—to complete the passage that I have just quoted. ' He that cometh to God must believe that He is, and that He is a rewarder of them that diligently seek Him.' (Heb. xi. 6.) Prayer involves faith.

And yet once more : it is a remarkable fact that perhaps in every place where prayer is made it is connected with the notion that he to Whom we pray has cause of offence against us, and that for this offence our life is forfeit to Him: that satisfaction must be made to Him for this offence before our prayer can be acceptable, or obtain from Him a favourable reply. Witness the offerings of blood, the sign of *life*, which, in all ages and over the face of nearly the whole earth, have accompanied and do still accompany the act of prayer. So far concerning prayer, man may know and thus much may he attain to, unassisted by the revealed Scripture, untaught by the Bible. But this is all; and what is it at the best? It is but a yearning desire, a trembling fear, a reaching forth into the dark, a faint glimmering of hope. So the wisest of the heathen have ever felt and confessed their prayers to be.

How different is prayer when we view it in the light of inspiration! how different to the Christian through the teaching that he has received in the clear revelation of God in Holy Scripture! Therein God has so revealed to us His glory and greatness and goodness and beauty, as to intensify our natural desire to pray. He offers Himself to our faith, as ready and willing to listen to us; and more!—stooping down to us in love unspeakable and infinite, and beseeching us to come to Him, the great Hearer of prayer. Our hope of an answer to prayer is *there*, confirmed by exceeding great and precious promises. *There*, the hindrances to the acceptance of prayer, dimly conjectured by nature, are clearly displayed before our eyes. The sinfulness of our fallen humanity and our actual transgressions, are shown in all the blackness of guilt with which they appear in the light of the holy, holy, holy God. But therein stands forth One fairer than the children of men, acceptable to God, taking all that guilt upon Himself. *There* we see how God Himself, in our nature, has become to His own justice the satisfaction for our offences, suffering for them on the cross; *there* we learn how by this expiation every barrier to our approach to God is taken away, so that in Christ Jesus we, who were once far off, are made nigh by His blood. In Him we have boldness and access with confidence by the faith of *Him* (i. e. by believing on *Him*, Eph. iii. 12), and are encouraged to 'come boldly to the throne of grace, that we may obtain mercy and find grace to help in time of need.' (Heb. iv. 16.)

When a man has with humble faith received the teaching of the Divine word, and has accepted the Saviour there set forth as his own Redeemer, as the one Mediator between him and his God, prayer becomes the habitual utterance of his soul. As often as God and eternity, and sin and duty, are the subject of his meditations, these meditations find expression in prayer. Whatever things of an earthly kind are so sanctified by the Holy Ghost as to lead his thoughts upward, those thoughts furnish occasion for prayer.

> 'Prayer is the Christian's vital breath,
> The Christian's native air;
> His watchword at the gates of death,
> He enters heaven by prayer.'

It is at once his duty and his privilege to live 'praying always,' as our text expresses it; that is, according to the original, praying in every season, on every occasion, at every opportunity; 'praying *always* with all prayer and supplication in the Spirit,'—with *every kind* of prayer.

I think that these words point out to us the difference between the prayer of the Christian and that of the unconverted man. The latter prays when he is in distress, the Christian prays on every occasion, with *every kind of prayer*— not only in the storm, but in the sunshine of prosperity, not only for the supply of his wants, but *with every kind of prayer*. The expression includes the presenting of our thankfulness, of our joy, of our love, of our adoration, of our delight in God our Saviour; *every kind of prayer* —as well 'Glory to God in the highest,' as 'God be merciful to me a sinner.' Christian prayer is the daily intercourse of a child with a beloved Parent. The Christian has received the Spirit of God's Son into his heart; but with him it is the Spirit of adoption, whereby he is enabled to cry 'Father!'

My brethren in Christ, how great the mercy that allows, that invites you thus to pray, and bids you pour into your Father's ear all that concerns you—each feeling of your hearts, each desire of your souls, laying all open before Him, that He may correct all that is wrong, and forgive it too, and bless that which is right, and lovingly sympathise with you in your sorrow and in your joy. How great the privilege of being allowed to pray on every occasion, with every kind of prayer and supplication—supplication for the relief of our own and our neighbours' necessities. While there are many kinds of prayer which are *not* supplication, yet we are to remember that in our sinful and dying state a great many of our prayers are and must be simple supplicating. Our necessities are so many and our weakness so great, our sins so frequent, that we cannot well enter into communion with God without speedily being reminded of the many things we need, and which He only can supply,—of our brethren's wants and our own.

Here I may notice a difficulty concerning the effect of this kind of prayer which often occurs to the man who views prayer by the light of nature alone. The feelings and desires of men are so opposite to each other that Christians may at the same time be asking for things which cannot *at once* be granted. Two nations are at war, and each prays for victory. How can *both* prayers be granted? Is the promise to hear prayer kept to the one side and broken to the other? I have noticed that this difficulty is sometimes put forward in the public newspapers. For instance, a bishop requests his clergy to pray for fair weather. At once he is blamed by some one who declares that a deluge of rain is the best thing that could happen for the health of the country, and bids us rather pray for its continuance. Supposing that these widely differing prayers were offered up, it is impossible that they could be literally answered at exactly the same time and place. The heathen of old perceived this difficulty, and in consequence represented prayer as sometimes in part, or altogether a failure, and its words scattered idly in the air. Holy Scripture teaches us a different lesson. It teaches us, and that most especially by our Saviour's example,—to pray, with a primary reference to the *glory of God*,—with humble submission to His will, and confidence in His wisdom and His love. And to pray for our fellow-Christians as well as for ourselves with regard to *their* need as well as to *our own*. They teach us that God never refuses to answer His servants' prayers, but that He grants them in His own time and way. The Christian prays as a child of God, as a member of the visible Church, and not for self alone. So Christ prayed, under pressure of impending agony and shame, with the dark day of Calvary in view. 'Father, save Me from this hour,' He cried. Then, reflecting that, should this prayer be granted, law would be unsatisfied and man unsaved, He adds. ' But for this cause came I unto this hour. Father, glorify Thy name.' (St. John, xii. 27. &c.) So at Gethsemane He prayed, ' Father, if Thou be willing, remove this cup from Me; nevertheless, *not My* will, but Thine be done.' The cup was not removed, but the prayer was heard, and the Lord's human nature was strengthened to fight the battle and to win the victory of life for us.

Brethren, ' Be careful for nothing, but in every thing by prayer and supplication with thanksgiving let your requests be made known unto God' (Phil. iv. 6), and leave Him to supply the answer as He will, and be sure of this, that the answer will be a blessing to you. And that your prayers may rise up with acceptance, seek for the Spirit of God to be in you, a spirit of prayer. Pray 'in the Spirit,' in the Spirit's influence, under the Spirit's guidance, with the Spirit's power and energy. Your prayers may rise from stammering lips, yet if they be the voice of the Holy Ghost in you, He that searcheth the hearts knoweth what those poor stammering lips would say, for He knoweth what is the mind of the Spirit. No prayer of His can fail. His voice in you will soar to the mercy-seat on high, and bring back a response that shall fill your heart with gratitude, and inspire your tongue with praise.

## XXIV.

### THE PUBLICAN'S FEAST.

St. Luke, v. 29.—'And Levi made Him a great feast in his own house: and there was a great company of publicans and of others that sat down with them.'

IT is often a very hard thing to convince a moral, respectable man that he is in God's sight a *sinner*, whose offences can only be expiated by the blood of a Divine Redeemer; a sinner who must be saved, if saved at all, upon the same terms with those on whom, from the pinnacle of his fancied worth and temporal respectability, he looks with scorn, as profligate and vile; a sinner whose nature is so radically corrupt that he must receive a right spirit, and be born again before he can be taken into God's family, and serve acceptably. Such persons compare themselves with the more openly sinful, and are flattered by their own apparent superiority: They need to apply to their moral stature the standard afforded in the Word of God, and exemplified in the man Christ Jesus; then they can form a true estimate of self, and be led to seek refuge in Christ. How long it took

Nicodemus to realise the truth of the Lord's teaching on these subjects, and openly and decidedly to range himself under the banner of the cross! 'Have any of the rulers, or of the Pharisees believed on Him?' (St. John, vii. 48) was the contemptuous question of the *reverend members of the Jewish Council* as to the *one* Saviour! (St. John, vii. 48.) 'God, I thank Thee that I am not as other men are, extortioners, unjust, adulterers, or even as this publican. I fast twice in the week, I give tithes of all that I possess' (St. Luke, xviii. 11, 12), cries the *Pharisee* in the parable. True, perhaps; yet this moral excellence was used by Satan to blind him to the state of his heart. On the other hand, those who had little earthly reputation, outward respectability, to hinder them, or who had no worldly morality on which to plume themselves, were often more ready to embrace the humbling terms on which God offers pardon, and to receive mercy joyfully at once. 'I am a sinful man, O Lord!' cried the poor *fisherman* (St. Luke, v. 8). 'God be merciful to me a sinner.' (St. Luke, xviii. 13,) burst from the publican in the parable. *Levi,* called by Christ, instantly 'left all, rose up, and followed him' (St. Luke, v. 28). 'And,' says our Lord to the chief priests and elders. 'the publicans and the *harlots* go into the Kingdom of God,' that is, embrace the Salvation of His Kingdom of Grace before you (St. Matt. xxi. 21). Yet we are not taught in Holy Scripture to undervalue moral worth and mere natural uprightness of character. On the other hand, it is shown us that, though Satan takes advantage of these qualities to keep men from coming to wash and be clean in a Redeemer's blood, yet that naturally moral and upright persons, when by grace enabled to cast themselves simply upon Christ crucified, do often become the most exemplary and consistent Christians. So it was in the case of the Pharisee, Saul of Tarsus. So also with Nicodemus, the dignified councillor.

When Levi, the converted publican, forsook Christ and fled along with the fishermen who at first had so readily followed Him,—the slow and reluctant Nicodemus came to Golgotha, and was not ashamed to honour the dead body of his Lord. The Saviour, in a wonderful manner, adapted his treatment of these two classes to their different characters. He impressed upon Nicodemus, (the outwardly moral and respectable man,) the necessity of a changed heart and salvation through grace; and this, in a long and authoritative discourse; while to the already humbled publicans, Zaccheus and Levi, He addressed the short but welcome invitations, 'Follow Me' (St. Luke, v. 27), and 'Zaccheus, make haste and come down, for to-day I must abide at thy house' (St. Luke, xix. 5). So also to the trembling and convicted woman He only says, 'Neither do I condemn thee; go and sin no more' (St. John, viii. 11). It is very interesting to notice in the Gospel history how often such as became His disciples offered that which was in their eyes the best they had to testify their love to the Saviour's person. Martha and Mary received Him into their house. Martha, the careful mistress of the family, served Him at supper. Mary, no doubt the younger sister, brought a woman's treasure, costly essence, and anointed His feet, and wiped them with her own hair (St. John, xii. 2). The publicans, Levi and Zacchens, rich men, accustomed to festivity, made each of them a feast for Him. The woman which was a sinner carried that which had been of value indeed to such as her for purposes of sin, and devoted it to the pitying Lord. It was an alabaster box of ointment, and she stood with it at His feet, behind Him weeping, and began to wash His feet with tears, and did wipe them with (her most prized adornment) the hair of her head, 'And kissed His feet, and anointed them with the ointment' (St. Luke, vii. 37, 38). The two great men, but late disciples themselves, highly valuing an honourable burial, offer, the one the spices for His embalming, the other his own new tomb 'which he had hewn out in the rock' (St. John, xix. 39, and St. Matt. xxvii. 40). The Lord suffers His dead body to lie in their reverent hands; for, you see, He never rejected any mark of love or gratitude shown to Him, even though to our minds it might seem beneath His dignity to accept it. When Levi made Him a great feast in his own house, Jesus accepted it as a proof of grateful love; and the cause of Levi's doing it was the mercy he had found in the 'joy of Salvation.' How glad he was! His spirit delighted in God his Saviour! He had given up the service of Mammon, the situation that brought him his money but led him into sin; he was henceforth to be a poor man,—to follow a Master who 'had not where to lay His head.' Those things which had been gain to him he had counted loss for Christ. Yet he was glad! In the days of his riches I daresay conscience had sorely tormented him. He knew that he was doing wrong; the fear of God's wrath weighed heavily on him, for he was a Jew and could not be ignorant of the requirements of God's law. Now he had risen up, left all, and followed the poor man of Nazareth. Yet he was glad: for it was the Messiah who had called him, and he had had grace to obey the call. *Now* he felt that, sinner as he had been, he was not a castaway; he was forgiven; and death, when it came, would not

be damnation, but the gate of life eternal. He
had lost the world, but had gained the salvation
of his soul. So he was glad. He might not as
yet be a very wise or advanced Christian, but he
loved the Lord who had called him. He had
been used to delight in a feast; it was the best
thing he could think of to offer; so he made a
great feast for Him in his own house, and *He*
came and sat down there. Compare Levi's
happiness with the misery of those who are conscious that they are sacrificing their souls for
the world's sake. Some are *consciously* losing
eternity for money or for business; the engross-
ing thought of which gives them little or no
time for the care of the soul. Some are given up
to a sinful conformity with the world: a sinful
lust, a sinful pursuit, a sinful love of idleness or
ease. Such know they are wrong, yet will not
ask help to be right, for they love their sin:
*they* cannot welcome Christ, there is no feast for
*Him* in their house. They are men of a *miserable*
spirit whenever they think of death, and judgment,
and eternity; but they are not men of a *broken*
and *contrite* spirit, and so the Lord will not dwell
with them. They go on hoping some day to
give up all that hinders Christ from coming to
them; some day, like Levi, to forsake all and
follow Him. What do they mean by *some day?*
They mean that they will give up sin, when they

THE PUBLICAN'S FEAST.

have got all they want by sin; they will hope to crucify a lust when they have worn it out, to resign the cup of worldly pleasure when they have quite emptied it; then they will receive Christ when He may have left off knocking at their door, and have passed by and gone for ever. Alas for them! No feast in *their* hearts, no Christ for their guest! The feast made for Him by Levi *was*, no doubt, a feast to our merciful Lord. As *man*, food was a refreshment and comfort to His body. The welcome of Levi, the society of so many who reverenced Him and hung upon the words of His lips; all these things were surely a feast to Him. Such a feast we cannot make for Him; the everlasting doors have lifted up themselves to receive Him. He sitteth at the right hand of the Father, and doth hunger and thirst no more; yet, brethren, He asks you to feast Him; He is waiting at the gate of each heart to be admitted. 'Behold,' He says, 'I stand at the door, and knock; if any man hear my voice, and open the door, I will come in to him, and will sup with him, and he with Me' (Rev. iii. 20). The same on the throne as on the earth, yesterday and to-day, for ever! But the feast *we* offer must be a purely spiritual feast. The opening of the door of the heart to receive Him as our Saviour from *sin;* the casting out of everything that occupies His supreme place, for the feast must be for *Him*; the offering of the soul, the thoughts and affections are to be *His*. This is the feast which we, too, can make for Him. A *great* feast; for so He condescends to consider it. He will enter in and partake thereof, and will 'see of the travail of His soul, and will be satisfied.' A very poor man can thus make a great feast for his Lord in his own house. Such a feast we make for Him in *His own house*, when we come with faith and repentance to the Holy Communion: there we offer and present unto Him ourselves, our souls and bodies, to be a reasonable, holy, and lively sacrifice unto Him. 'We be not worthy,' our Church reminds us, 'to offer Him any sacrifice:' and yet a living sacrifice, this He will not despise. And if you would offer to Him any *material* feast, you may, in one sense, do it. Have you heard His call and obeyed it? Then will He accept you, if, for His sake, you feast the sick, the aged, and the really poor. Of such a feast He will one day say, 'Ye have done it unto Me.'

Finally, brethren, consider the earthly guests at this great feast: a great company of publicans and sinners, Levi (or St. Matthew) calls them, in his Gospel, (chapter ix. 10,) strange guests to invite to meet Christ. But oh, Christian people, Levi had been a publican himself; he knew what it was to want a Saviour; he had heard from *Jewish* teachers that repentance was impossible for such as him. He had been desperate till that loving voice of the sinless Lord had called to him and said to him 'Follow Me;' and so he could not but bring his fellow-sinners to meet the same Lord. The joy of salvation is no selfish joy. He who has felt the love of Christ for *himself*, and *knows* the love of Christ for *others*, and has drank in of the Spirit of Christ, he is filled with Christ's love for souls. He cannot refrain from inviting others to come and meet the same Saviour; and this he does by personal effort, by self-denial, by prayer. Going himself, or, by his contributions, helping to send others into the highways and hedges, and compelling men to come in. You, brethren, if any are here, who are angry at the encouragement given by Christ's ministers to sinners to come in and accept His salvation, and feast upon it; do *you* remember this publican's feast, and how the Pharisees taunted our Lord with His company, and how He replied to them; 'They that are whole, need not a physician, but they that are sick. I came not to call the righteous, but sinners to repentance' (St. Luke, v. 31, 32). It *must* have been a happy feast, brethren. The chief guest the Saviour, rejoicing in Spirit over penitent Levi and his company; the publicans and sinners rejoicing at the gracious words of mercy that proceeded out of His mouth; Levi rejoicing in God his Saviour, and in hope that his fellow-sinners might find Him *theirs*. Angels silently hovering over the company, and joying over each penitent there. O you that have rejected such a feast, not literal but spiritual, I do in Christ's name invite each one of you; 'for,' saith our glorified Lord, 'Whosoever will, let him take the water of life *freely*.'

## XXV.

### THE LORD SHOWING TO MAN HIS THOUGHT.

Amos, iv., part of verse 13.—'He declareth unto man what is His thought.'\*

IN a solemn message to Israel, the Lord enumerates, by His prophet, the judgments inflicted upon that people, as warnings to repentance. For the great national sin of idolatry, for their cruel oppression of the poor and needy, for their luxury and self-indulgence, He had chastised them with famine and drought, with blasting and mildew, with the pestilence and with the sword. Many of them He had cut off; some He had rescued as brands already kindled, but snatched from the burning. 'Yet,' he adds, 'yet, have ye not returned unto me.' Judgment and mercy alike despised, once again the voice of God gives notice of the coming

---

\* I have followed Scott and Wordsworth as to the sense of this verse, and also, I think, the meaning of our Authorised Version. But the Septuagint reads, 'Ἀπαγγέλλων εἰς ἀνθρώπους τὸν Χριστὸν αὐτοῦ: and the Douay version, 'declareth His word to man.'

outburst of His wrath, of the out-pouring of judgments yet more severe, warning them to make ready for the trial. 'Because I will do this unto thee, prepare to meet thy God, O Israel.' Then follows that magnificent description of Himself by God, from which I have taken the text, 'He that formeth the mountains, and createth the wind, and declareth unto man his thought, that maketh the morning darkness, that treadeth upon the high places of the earth, The Lord, The God of Hosts, is His name.'

'He declareth unto man what is His thought.' Our first inference from these words naturally is, in the language of Scripture, 'The Lord *knoweth* the thoughts of man.' How little do we realise this truth, and, in consequence, how little restraint do we exercise over our thoughts! We may be careful in our *doings*, we may even try, by God's help, to watch over our *words*, but our thoughts, the action of the highest part of man, the workings of the immortal *soul*,—brethren, how often do we suffer them to wander ungoverned, to indulge in vanity, to exercise themselves in sin! Who among us would be willing that his thoughts should be *written out*, and *published* for his neighbours to read,—his thoughts of envy and wrath, of pride and lust, of discontent and covetousness, his evil thoughts of other men, his thoughts of selfishness? How few thoughts of our Creator, Preserver, Redeemer, and Sanctifier! How few thoughts for His service and glory! Indeed, God is not in all our thoughts. And our neighbours, how little charity is in our thoughts for *them*, how much jealousy, how scant the pity, how cold the love! How different, too, are our thoughts from our professions! So that we seem to realise the saying of a very clever, but very wicked, statesman, who said that words were given us to hide our thoughts. What would our neighbours think of us could they read our thoughts, *all* our thoughts? But though they cannot read our thoughts, yet by our side all day and all night long is a *presence*, unseen, but real, a *Watcher* Whom nothing can escape; over us, all day and all night long, is an Eye that slumbereth not, nor sleepeth. *That Presence* is *among* our thoughts, *that Eye* beholds every feeling, every affection, every desire. The presence is the presence of Jehovah, the eye is the eye of the pure and the holy One. All these thoughts of ours are observed by Him; not one forgotten; all to be unfolded in the day of judgment.

I know, brethren, that many of us are earnestly trying, by the grace of God, to rule and govern our thoughts, to put away from us evil thoughts, to cultivate habits of holy and charitable thought, of pure, true, and humble thought; yet even when so trying, how often do we relax our efforts, how often are we overcome by the deceitfulness of our own hearts, how often do we suffer vain thoughts to lodge within us! It is an unspeakable mercy that the believer in Christ may look to His blood to atone for his evil thoughts ; that he may claim, in prayer, the promise of the Holy Spirit, to enable him daily to watch, and finally to be more than conqueror, over his own sinful heart, that 'every thought may be brought into captivity to the obedience of Christ.'

The Christian man, thus living, thus trusting in the atonement made by Christ, conscious that in the power of the Holy Ghost he is so striving against inward sinfulness, may exercise a strange and wonderful privilege. He may dare to lay open his thoughts before God, to call God's attention to them, to sanctify them. 'Search me, O God, and know my heart, try me, and know my thoughts, and see if there be any wicked way in me, and lead me in the way everlasting.' (Ps. cxxxix. 23, 24.) So prayed David in his repentance, when indulgence in vile imaginings had led him into sin that disquieted the rest of his life, and brought him under most heavy chastisement. So, our Church teaches us to pray at the commencement of our Communion service, 'Cleanse the thoughts of our hearts, by the inspiration of Thy Holy Spirit.'

Further, brethren, the sincere Christian has in his heart, by grace working in him, *some* thoughts, which it is to him a great delight to remember are known to his God; as he meditates on the Word of God, as he lifts up his soul in prayer and praise, though his hands may be busy in necessary toil, and his lips be silent, yet he is glad to be sure that God knows these thoughts of his, and holds through them communion with him, and sees in them the fruit of His own Spirit. Especially is it a matter for rejoicing and adoration to him to be assured that the Almighty mind, embracing at once time and eternity, earth, heaven, and infinity, is occupied about *him*, rejoicing in *his* sanctified affections, and listening, well pleased, as he lays bare his poor, sinful heart before Him. That his God is acquainted with his thoughts, as he looks up to Him and cries, 'Lord, Thou knowest all things, all my sins, negligences, and ignorances, all my wandering and evil thoughts; Thou knowest all things, Thou knowest that I love Thee.'

We are reminded in the text that He who thus knows the thoughts of man also declares to man what they are. He declares to man the thoughts themselves, and shows him of what kind they are. He teaches them to discern between good and evil thoughts, between those that are the fruits of the Spirit and such as proceed from the corrupt fountain of the natural heart. And this He is pleased to do in different ways and for various purposes. Thus, when He came down upon earth, He declared unto the Jews and Scribes and Pharisees their sinful thoughts concerning Himself. He did this in such a way as to show them the evil of their thoughts, and to afford a convincing proof of His own Godhead. Seeing the faith of some who brought to Him a sick man to be healed, he says to him, 'Son, be of good cheer, thy sins be forgiven thee.' And certain of the scribes 'said within themselves, This man blasphemeth.' The all-seeing God is manifested in *His* answer to their thoughts. 'Jesus, knowing their thoughts, said, Wherefore think ye evil in your hearts? For whether is easier to say, Thy sins be forgiven thee; or to say, Arise, and walk?' Then He gives them a practical reply to His own question, and proves Himself to be the Lord, able to forgive sins, by saying to the sick man, 'Arise, take up thy bed, and go unto thine house.' And the palsied creature, till then unable to move, touched by the word of Divine power, at once rises up whole, and departs to his home (St. Matt. ix. 7). On another occasion, when they were watching Him to see whether He would heal on the Sabbath day, that they might have an accusation against Him, He proves His divinity by declaring to them their thoughts, and replying to them in the question, 'Is it lawful on the Sabbath day to do good or to do evil, to save life, or to destroy it?' (St. Luke, vi. 7.)

And as He answered the thoughts of His enemies, so did He reply to those of His disciples. When He had said to them, 'A little while and ye shall not see Me, and again a little while and ye shall see Me, because I go to the Father,' the disciples began to inquire among themselves what these words could mean. Jesus, knowing their *desire*, replies to their unspoken question with such an explanation of His saying that they are at once led to ascribe to Him omniscience, the attribute of God alone, and to acknowledge His mission from the Father. 'Now are we sure that Thou knowest all things, and needest not that any man should ask Thee: by this we believe that Thou camest forth from God.' (St. John, xvi. 16, &c.) To pass by numerous instances of a similar kind, I call your attention to one most interesting example, where our Lord declareth to a man his thoughts, so as at once to show His gracious approval of those thoughts, and, as in the other examples, to manifest His

Godhead. In a retired spot in Galilee, beneath the shadow of a fig-tree, there stands a sincere and true-hearted man, in solitary communion with his God. No human eye beholds, no human ear can hear him. His thoughts are answered by the arrival of a friend who leads Him to the Redeemer. *He* welcomes him with the words, 'Behold an Israelite indeed, in whom is no guile. How knowest Thou me?' cries the astonished man. 'Before that Philip called thee, when thou wast under the fig-tree, I saw thee.' Such testimony Nathaniel could not resist. 'Rabbi, Thou art the "Son of God."' (St. John, i. 43, &c.)

'He declareth unto man what is his thought.' He does this by His holy Word, so as to prove that Word to be the Word of God,—a living word exercising a living power,—and at the same time to produce in man conviction of sin, or to speak peace and comfort to his soul, according to his need. 'The Word of God is quick (living), and powerful, and sharper than any two-edged sword, piercing even to the dividing asunder of soul and spirit, and of the joints and marrow, and is a discerner of the thoughts and intents of the heart.' (Heb. iv. 12.) How many a careless sinner has been arrested in his downward road by this living word, used by the Holy Ghost to disclose to him the secrets of his soul, and to declare to him of what kind they are — how offensive to the Almighty, how poisonous to himself, how ruinous for eternity! And then, as he has gone on his way in silent grief and terror, saying in his heart, 'What shall I do to be saved?' how has that word, as with a living voice, declared to him God's knowledge of his thought, and God's answer to it, in such a promise as, 'Believe on the Lord Jesus Christ, and thou shalt be saved!' And when the voice of his soul has been, 'Lord, I believe, help Thou mine unbelief,' again has his thought been met, and its acceptance declared to him, in the reply of the word, impressed with living energy upon his heart, 'Son, be of good cheer, thy sins be forgiven thee.'

Finally, brethren, let us realise that God will declare unto man what are His thoughts at the last day. The day when He shall bring every work into judgment, with every secret thing, whether it be good or whether it be evil. Wherefore 'Prepare to meet thy God;'—not a God to whom good and evil are indifferent, a God easy and indulgent to sin, as some dare think. To them He declares their thought;—'Thou thoughtest that I was such an one as thyself: but I will reprove thee, and set' these things that thou hast done 'in order before thine eyes.' (Ps. l. 21.) And, yet, a God who will never lay upon man the guilt of thought, word, or deed, if only he be found at the foot of the cross, casting his sins' burden upon a dying Lord.

## XXVI.

#### THE DEATH OF THE RIGHTEOUS.

'And he died.'—GEN. v. 27.

SUCH, in all probability, will be the close of our history here on earth. In many other particulars there is a wide difference between us. As to fortune, rank, talents, strength, wealth, length of days, you can scarcely say anything of one of us that would be equally suitable and true if asserted of another. To one all of these things seem to be granted by the providence of God; to another, few, if any, of them are given. Some of us are full of joy and happiness, while others 'mourn and weep.' Some rest and are at peace, while others toil and struggle all their days. But *one* thing happens alike to all, and *will* probably happen alike to us all. All are of the dust, and all turn to dust again. (Eccles. xii. 7:) 'And the spirit shall return unto God Who gave it.' I say probably, for mankind shall not all sleep. The day, the last day, is coming.

which will find the world full of busy, living men ; yet, except that day come first, you and I are going to die.

Brethren, how soon we none of us can tell. How do we feel as to the prospect ? Death in itself is not a happy subject of contemplation ; nay, to my mind death is rightly termed the 'king of terrors.' In the word of God, death is spoken of as an enemy—the 'last enemy that shall be destroyed.' Shall we then treat death as an unavoidable evil ? Shall we, so far as we can, put away the thought of death from us ? Shall we try to be deaf to his advancing step, that sounds in our ears each time the clock strikes ? Shall we blind our eyes to the awful shadow that comes nearer with every setting sun; until that footfall be heard at our own door, that shadow enfold us in the darkness of our last night ? Is the control of death in the hands of an inflexible fate, or of a cruel tyrant, or of a blind chance ? Must we look upon it as that man of old looked up at the sword suspended by a single hair just over his head ? Or is it possible in any way so to alter the conditions of death as to change the aspect under which it presents itself to our eyes, and to enable us to look upon it with unflinching, even with hopeful gaze, as a happy though a deeply solemn event. Can we by any means prevail to have the sword that hangs over all taken down from above our heads, and placed in the hands of a friend, so that we may be sure that the inevitable stroke will be inflicted in the best way and at the best time for us?

These are questions of deep personal interest to us all, brethren; the heathen in old times so considered them. In more than one country it was their custom to call death to remembrance by having the image of a corpse carried round the table at their feasts. By some this seems to have been done that the guests might be warned so to live as they would wish they had lived when they came to die. The inference drawn from the custom by others was this, Let us eat and drink, for to-morrow we die. How does God regard this subject? 'And he died.' A strange, short record appended to the memorial given of each of the antediluvian patriarchs descended of the family of Seth. Now, we may notice of this family that it was the race destined to be the heirs of the promise, the race from which God the Son was Himself to derive His human nature,—a race amongst whom were to be found such saints as Enoch and Noah. We cannot be mistaken in taking this race as the type of the church of God, and it is more than probable that the church of God was only to be found among them. *Their* deaths are recorded by God; of the deaths of the family of Cain, the type of the world, of the ungodly, no record is given, no notice taken.

We see, then, that there is a death which God thinks worth recording; there is about it something of value. He esteems it as not an evil unmixed, but rather as that in which the good so far outweighs the evil that He will not have it forgotten. 'Precious in the sight of the Lord is the death of His saints.' (Psa. cxv. 15.) It may be in order to hinder us from putting off our repentance and faith in Christ to a dying day that so little is said in Holy Scripture of the circumstances attending the departure of the servants of God to the next world. The word of God does not dwell upon death-bed scenes; yet whenever a more particular description is given of the death of a man of faith, it is astonishing to see how different an aspect death presents to us from that in which it is looked upon by mankind in general. *How* did these men die? Consider the death-bed of Jacob the patriarch. Hear him 'when the time drew near that Israel must die;' hear him call his sons together, and with holy rapture pronounce the Divine decision as to their future destiny, that which should befall them in the last days. Where is the fear of death? In the midst of his prophetic utterance the remembrance of his approaching departure comes over him, but he welcomes it as the long-expected deliverance, and breaks forth into the exulting cry, 'I have waited for Thy salvation, O Lord.' 'And when Jacob had made an end of commanding his sons, he gathered up his feet into the bed, and yielded up the ghost, and was gathered to his people.' (Gen. xlix. 33.) Behold Aaron and Moses, as each in turn calmly ascends the mountain prescribed by God, and without one cry of terror or alarm resigns his spirit into his Maker's hands. Regard the close of David's eventful life. Listen to his last public address to his subjects: 'Now bless the Lord your God;' then, 'he died in a good old age, full of days, riches, and honour.' (1 Chron. xxix. 20, 28.)

It is an ancient fancy, I know not if it be true, that when it grows old and feels the approach of death, the swan, mute before or uttering only a harsh cry, pours forth a song of surpassing melody. Hear the swanlike song of aged Simeon as, with that wondrous Child enfolded in his arms, he sings his dying strain: 'Lord, now lettest Thou Thy servant depart in peace.' (St. Luke, ii. 29.) There is no dread of death here.

But it may be said you have chosen instances of men who died a peaceful death in the fulness of their age; like weary travellers they laid

s

them down to rest at the end of life's journey. We wonder not so much at the calmness of their departure. But *we* may be cut off by a violent death, a death of agonizing pain. *We* may be called away in our prime, and the cup of happiness, such as earth can give, may be snatched from our lips, ere we have well tasted of its sweetness. Can *such* a death be calmly met? Can living man descend peacefully into an untimely grave? What is that crowd doing? Hark to their cries and execrations as they drag their unresisting victim along the streets, and hurl him forth at the city gate. Let us press forward and look at him. Painful as it may be, let us get one glance at his pale, horror-stricken face. Stay! what is this? There is no terror there. It is as the face of one who never knew fear or felt pain; as the face of an angel. They are battering him to death with stones; yet look once more. His eye is fixed on something you and I cannot see; on some One to Whom he is speaking. What is he saying? Does he cry in agony for life and deliverance? 'Lord, lay not this sin to their charge. And when he had said this, he fell asleep.' (Acts, vii. 60.) This man was in the full vigour of life and usefulness. 'Let me die the death of the righteous, and let my last end be like his!' (Num. xxiii. 10.)

Does any one here say, You have been

showing us how good men can die; to such, I grant, death may not be an unwelcome visitor; but I have not been a good man. In whatever way these men escaped the terror of death, I have not walked in it yet ; can I find that way ? I cannot bear the thought of dying, yet my sun of life may soon set. Can I find that light at eventide, or must I face the king of terrors in despair ? It was not their goodness that enabled these men to die so well. But for *thee*, my fellow-sinner, I have comfort,—One dying, and only one, from whom thou too mayest derive encouragement. Come to the three crosses, on either side one, and Jesus in the midst. On one of the outer crosses there is dying in pain a man who, till an hour ago, was a hardened criminal and a blasphemer of his Lord. Since then he has repented and believed in that dying One by his side, and confessed his sin and justified his Saviour. Hear him ! There is no sound of terror in that low, pleading voice, 'Lord, remember me.' No sentence of despair in the reply, 'To-day shalt thou be with Me in Paradise.' (St. Luke, xxiii. 43.) The dying thief, looking on a dying Saviour, hath conquered the fear of death, as well as the dying martyr who expires gazing on Jesus standing at the right hand of God.

'And he died.' Was there no terror in his

death? Here is the reason;—'for whom Christ died.' (1 Cor. viii. 11.) The patriarchs looked forward to a promised, as we look backward to an accomplished, atonement. 'The sting of death is sin,' and Christ put away sin by the sacrifice of Himself. Not only did He bear our sin, its guilt, its punishment, but *put it away*. Dying, the believer may exclaim, 'Who is he that condemneth? It is Christ that died.' If we have accepted Christ, if we will to-day accept Christ, why should we fear to die? Why should *we* avoid the mention of death? God thinks it good to record of each member of a whole age of His servants, 'And he died.' Christ, the Man Christ Jesus, hath tasted death for every man, and death could not conquer *Him*. 'He died;' but we hear a voice from Him, saying, 'I am He that liveth, and was dead, and, behold, I am alive for evermore;' and we remember His words, 'Because I live ye shall live also.' Having conquered him that had the power of death, that power is now His. He now, by virtue of that power, reserves to Himself the office of taking His people home (Rev. xiv. 14, 16). It is His to regulate the time, the mode, the circumstances of their death.

Oh, Christian people, it is a very solemn thing to have to die. Yet if death be in His hands, we should not look on death with terror.

To them that are His, death is gain. It is freedom from sin, and from temptation to sin, for ever. It is freedom from all that can pain or annoy or affright. 'The righteous is taken away from that which is evil.' saith Isaiah (lvii. 1, margin). It is the end of struggling and of toil. 'They shall rest in their beds.' (Isa. lvii. 2.) It is not sleep, but resting life: 'each one walking in his uprightness.' (Ibid.) It is the exchange of that which is good—Christian life here—for that which is far, *very far* better,—Christian life in the immediate presence of God and in the visible companionship of the Lord Jesus Christ. To them that are *His*, death is gain. How can we realise this each one for himself? By seeking grace of the Holy Ghost, and then striving in strength of that grace to live *near* to Christ, to become *like* Christ, *close* to Christ: in constant, simple, single reliance on His blood that cleanseth us from all sin: near Him in continual, instant prayer, in the study of His word and meditation thereon, in the means of grace which He hath ordained, in the holy Communion of His body and His blood. *Like* Him in living for our Father's service and our Father's glory; *like* Him in pureness of heart; *like* Him in love and charity, in temper, in word, and in earnest, holy, self-denying life. So may 'we have boldness, because as *He* is so are we in this world.'

(1 St. John, iv. 17.) So will the fear of death be taken away, so shall we be enabled as our dying hour draws near to cry, ' O death, where is thy sting ? O grave, where is thy victory ?' (1 Cor. xv. 55.)

## XXVII.

#### THE LIGHT OF THE BLESSED.

Rev. xxii. 5, first clause.—'There shall be no night there.'

MY brethren, I have no doubt these words have a literal meaning, applicable to that home of glory, wherein the redeemed Church of God shall dwell for ever and ever. The division of time, the flight of those hours, of which it is so truly said 'they perish,' but which will leave their record, will not *then* be marked by the alternations of day and night. The gradual brightening of the dawn, the calmer glories of the setting sun, the deep obscurity of the dark, will all be unknown, for 'There shall be no night there.'

This declaration would be no good news to us in our present state. While night has its dangers and its trials, yet how greatly are they surpassed by its blessings! For night brings rest and refreshment to wearied bodies, and often over-laden minds. How sweet is the hour of darkness to him who has toiled conscientiously till set of sun, and who then lays down wearied limbs, committing himself to that Keeper of His people, Who neither slumbers nor sleeps. How blessed the calm night to the brain, aching from intellectual toil, and to him whose days are days of mourning, or of care! How beautiful the prayer our Church hath taught her children as night closes in! 'Lighten our darkness, we beseech Thee, O Lord!' Great are the blessings of the night! Yet who of us all remembers to give thanks, because daylight does not invite us unceasingly to toil and anxiety; to sing, 'O ye nights, bless ye the Lord; O darkness, bless the Lord; praise Him and magnify Him for ever.'

But, brethren, if we think upon the subject, we shall see that the blessings of the night are all connected with a state of trouble, labour, and imperfection. Hence we may understand there being in heaven no time of sleep and darkness. If rest be sweet to the weary, forgetfulness to the sorrowing, sweeter far will it be to the redeemed, never to be weary again, to sorrow no more, for ever! In that world, sin, care, and suffering, will be of the past. None will feel the need of rest or of forgetfulness. Wakeful through eternity, they will live to glorify their King, 'And there shall be no night there.' But our text has also a figurative meaning.

I believe that this collect, 'Lighten our darkness,' is not alone a prayer against dangers of literal night, but for deliverance from the perils of a state of which night is a figure and foreshadowing. So in the text, night is a picture of the condition of this world, physical, moral, and intellectual. Of human nature, darkened by the fall, violated by sin; of ignorance, of watching, of mourning, and of dying; all suggested by that word *night*. Even in material science our highest attainments are but glimmerings, guesses at truth. And in spiritual things, to *nature* all is obscure, a darkness that may be felt. Sin, like a black cloud, broods over the face of the earth, sin and all the woes it has brought in its train.

For centuries we have been trying to light up a dark world, and trying in vain. Despite the earnest efforts of statesmen and philosophers, I fear the amount of guilt and misery, *that* darkness which overhangs our race, has been little if at all diminished, where we have been unblessed by Gospel influence. There *is* indeed a light come into the world, but it shineth in a *dark* place 'Ye are not in darkness,' says St. Paul to Christians; yet the same Apostle declares, '*Now* we see through a glass *darkly*.' There is a light come into the world, as bright as men could bear to look upon; a lamp to our feet, a guide to that place where darkness shall be over.

'I am the light of life,' says Christ, 'the true light,' the light that shines in Old and New Testaments, and most brightly from the cross. But the bulk of men, to whom that Light is offered, admire its lustre, and turn away from it. It is pleasant news to many, that Christ died to save sinners, that His sufferings were the punishment due to their sins, that His righteousness is accepted by God, in the place of what they could not offer; that they have only to believe this, to plead it with God, and they shall be saved. But when told that all this was to bring them *near to God*, to enable them 'to deny ungodliness and worldly lusts, to make them live, not to themselves, but to God,' then, brethren, the greater number turn from the light and plunge back into the darkness. Woe's me! *eternal* darkness; for 'this is the condemnation, that light is come into the world, and men loved darkness rather than light, because their deeds were evil.' Some there are who do humbly and thankfully accept that light, who try to walk in it, to follow the example of Him who has saved them. Their path shineth more and more; yet even with them it is very far from being 'perfect day.' They *have light*, but it is to guide them through *darkness*, for life here is, and must be, *this night* to the Christian, though he sees afar off the rising of the dawn. He is here, in much ignorance of God's character, works and ways. They are gloriously displayed in Christ; yet he beholds even Christ only by faith, and the faith is dim. And many a vapour of sin and infirmity intervenes between his upward gaze and the Lord he desires to look upon. He knows enough to save him, but not enough to satisfy him.

God's dispensations are full of mystery; God's dealings in his own case are often a trial to his belief. How many an enigma he has to solve with these words, 'Clouds and darkness are round about Him,' but 'righteousness and judgment are the habitation of His throne;' 'shall not the Judge of all the earth do right?' He is ignorant, too, of his fellow-servants; how little do Christians know of each other, as Christians; how little of each other's trials and difficulties! How often they misunderstand and, through misunderstanding, misrepresent each other! Many a disciple is unknown to his brethren, or, as in St. Paul's case, at the outset, is not believed by them to be a disciple. *Here*, indeed, we see through a glass darkly; but *then* all will be changed, and we shall see 'face to face.' Here 'we know in part, but then shall we know even as also we are known;' 'there shall be no night there.' But again, Satan tempts the Christian to doubt the love of God, the truth of God, and the word of God, and to question whether He is really in a state of salvation. At times he feels in much darkness through these temptations; almost lost. True, he carries his doubts in prayer to his Father in heaven and, confessing their sinfulness, seeks and finds, rest from them. But how far more blessed will be that place where doubt will be impossible, and perplexity dispelled for ever! for 'There shall be no night there.' Here the Christian stands as an armed and watchful sentinel in the obscurity of night. He never can tell from which direction the enemy will approach, on which side the next assault will be made. He dares not relax his vigilance, for he is sure that invisible foes hover in the darkness around. If they find him off his guard they will wound his conscience, and hinder his usefulness, lead him into sin, and even compass his destruction. But he looks forward with hope to that world, whence these enemies will be driven back by the unclouded brightness of the Sun of Righteousness; for 'There shall be no night there!'

Once more the Christian's life on earth is darkened by frequent mourning, and by death. Fears dim his vision, friends pass out of his reach, he beholds them no more! He knows where they are (if Christians), but the loss is bitter. And he himself looks down into the grave; it will end *his* work for Christ, and any labours of love for man. He knows his Saviour conquered the grave, and will not leave *him* there. He knows that there is eternal brightness for him beyond the grave; and yet is it a dark bourne for ourselves, or for those we love. But there are no graves, no funerals, in heaven; for there shall be no more sorrow, nor sighing, nor any night there.

What is it that in that world shall disperse the darkness? What radiant fount of light shall fill every soul with brightness, and illumine with eternal glory the mansions of the blessed? The answer is given in Rev. xxi. 23: 'The Lamb is the Light thereof.'

Thousands of thousands of bright forms walk the streets of the heavenly city ; yet is theirs but reflected light. He, and He only, is the source of all the light; in His presence night may not be, and Christians there behold Him, and are changed into His likeness. He is the brightness of the Father's glory. They see Him clearly, and they know Him as they are known. In the enlightened understanding of His works and ways, in the unclouded contemplation of His character and attributes, all difficulties and doubts disperse, and every mystery is unfolded. Understanding Him, Christians understand each other, for all resemble Him. The darkness of sorrow is gone, for He 'wipes away all tears from their eyes,' and the gloom of death has fled, for death himself is destroyed.

Seeing then, my brethren, that we look for such things,— or must I say *if* 'we look for such things, what manner of persons ought we to be?' What kind of life ought we to lead? The patriarchs of old, who sought the same 'better country,' confessed by their lives that they were strangers and pilgrims upon earth. Can we expect to join them above and yet live, as too many of us do, as if this world were our all? Talking of heaven, and living for earth, professing to love God, yet setting affection on things below, giving our nominal allegiance to the Lamb, the Light of heaven, but our real service to 'the ruler of the darkness of this world?'

Brethren, pray for the Holy Ghost to make you more in earnest; to arouse them that are not at all in earnest. Let us seek grace to walk in the light of faith *now*; so only shall we reach that place of which it is said 'There shall be no night there.'

www.ingramcontent.com/pod-product-compliance
Lightning Source LLC
Chambersburg PA
CBHW031929230426
43672CB00010B/1860